PERSPECTIVES ON
NOTATION AND PERFORMANCE

The *Perspectives of New Music* Series

Perspectives on American Composers
Perspectives on Contemporary Music Theory
Perspectives on Notation and Performance
Perspectives on Schoenberg and Stravinsky, Revised

PERSPECTIVES ON NOTATION AND PERFORMANCE

Edited by

Benjamin Boretz and Edward T. Cone

W · W · NORTON & COMPANY · INC ·

NEW YORK

Library of Congress Cataloging in Publication Data

Main entry under title:

Perspectives on notation and performance.

"Essays . . . reprinted from issues of Perspectives of new music."
1. Musical notation. 2. Music—Performance.
3. Music—History and criticism—20th century.
I. Boretz, Benjamin. II. Cone, Edward T.
III. Perspectives of new music.
ML431.P47   781'.24   75-31887
ISBN 0-393-02190-4
ISBN 0-393-00809-6 pbk.

The following essays are reprinted from issues of *Perspectives of New Music,* a journal published twice yearly by Perspectives of New Music, Inc., and copyrighted in the years indicated by Perspectives of New Music, Inc:

American Performance and New Music; Problems and Methods of Notation; The Changing Composer-Performer Relationship: A Monologue and a Dialogue; the Performer's Point of View: © 1963.

Notes on the Performance of Contemporary Music: © 1964

Note Values; What Indeterminate Notation Determines; Preparing Stockhausen's *Momente*; Notation—Material and Form: © 1965

Notation in General—Articulation in Particular; For the Flute: A List of Double-Stops, Triple-Stops, Quadruple-Stops, and Shakes: © 1966

A Descriptive Language for the Analysis of Electronic Music; Programmed Signals to Performers: A New Compositional Resource: © 1967

On Violin Harmonics; Graphical Language for the Scores of Computer-Generated Sounds; Some Multiple-Sonorities for Flute, Oboe, Clarinet, and Bassoon: © 1968

Notation for Piano; The Flute: New Sounds: © 1972

ACKNOWLEDGMENTS

Associated Music Publishers, Inc., New York. Brown: *Hodograph*, Copyright 1961; Carter: *Double Concerto*, Copyright 1962 and 1964; String Quartet No. 2, Copyright 1961; *Variations for Orchestra*, Copyright 1957; Castiglioni: *Tropi*, Copyright 1960 by Edizioni Suvini Zerboni, Milan; Cowell: *Fabric*, Copyright 1922, 1950 by Breitkopf Publications, New York; Kirchner: Concerto for violin, cello, ten winds, and percussion, Copyright 1962.

Bärenreiter Verlag, Kassel. Krenek: *Sechs Vermessene*, Copyright 1960.

McGinnis and Marx, New York. Evangelisti: *Proiezioni Sonore*, Copyright 1961 by Edition Tonos, Darmstadt; Wolpe: Quartet for oboe, cello, piano, and percussion, Copyright 1958.

Oxford University Press, Inc., New York. Ghent: *Dithyrambos*, Copyright 1968.

C. F. Peters Corporation, New York. Cage: *Music of Changes I* and *IV*, Copyright 1961 by Henmar Press, New York.

Theodore Presser Co., Bryn Mawr. Babbitt: *Composition for Four Instruments*, Copyright 1948 by New Music Edition; Berg: Violin Concerto, Copyright 1936; Boulez: *Improvisation sur Mallarmé (Une dentelle s'abolit* and *Le vierge)*, Copyright 1958; Third Piano Sonata, Copyright 1961; Haubenstock-Ramati: *Séquences*, Copyright 1961; Stockhausen: *Klavierstücke*, Copyright 1954 by Universal Edition, London.

PREFACE

HUGO RIEMANN, in his quirky but valuable *Musikalische Dynamik und Agogik* (Hamburg and St. Petersburg, 1884), adduces an instructive example of the complementary relation between notation and performance—a controversial example, to be sure, but one that is at the least highly suggestive. Riemann claims that our standard notation fails to give an accurate picture of a common rhythmic situation. Provocatively, he argues (p. 75) that such a configuration as the following, involving a triplet upbeat motif,

[musical notation example]

is really a substitute ("vikarirende") notation for a more exact version:

[musical notation example]

In this case the alteration is easy enough, but in actual compositions strict adherence to Riemann's suggested emendations would complicate many apparently simple passages. According to his analysis (p. 240), Chopin's Mazurka Op. 24, No. 2, mm. 5–6, now written thus:

[musical notation example]

should be understood as:

[musical notation example]

And the Nocturne Op. 9, No. 2, m. 18, now:

[musical notation example]

stands for:

[musical notation example]

Riemann insists that "these problematical rhythmic constructions are to be articulated as far as possible with reference to the motifs replaced by the substitute notation." Moreover, "in many cases, at least, it may happen that those motivic constructions are quite perceptible and that no exact notation exists for them" (p. 242). Riemann's point is easily grasped: our notation of metrical sub-division is based on the unity of the beat and of the measure. Rhythmic motifs are therefore visually presented in "downbeat" form ("anbetont"); nevertheless, many of them embody "upbeat" gestures ("abbetont") or even straddle the pulse ("inbetont"). It is up to the performer to make these distinctions clear in the face of an imprecise text.

Whether Riemann is right or wrong in these specific instances, he certainly draws attention to a major shortcoming of our nota-tion: its failure to clarify rhythmic as opposed to metric units. And despite the occasional use by individuals of various symbolic devices—including some of Riemann's own—there has so far been surprisingly little progress toward correcting that situation. In the present volume, for example, there is much discussion of difficul-ties of "rhythmic" notation: how certain patterns are to be set down and how others, set down in greater or lesser detail, are to be played. Yet almost every case reduces the rhythmic problem to the narrowly durational: exactly when is a note to be attacked, exactly how long is it to be sustained? Virtually no attention is paid to the vastly more complex—one might almost say more basic—question of rhythmic grouping. Indeed, some of the authors may appear to denigrate its importance—although for valid heuristic reasons: witness, for example, Gunther Schuller's re-writing of pseudo-Stockhausen (p. 5) and Charles Wuorinen's of Morley (p. 53–54).

Now, it is obvious that musicians of the stature of Schuller and Wuorinen cannot really be uninterested in one of the funda-mental problems of articulation. Riemann is by no means alone in his awareness of the actual rhythmic structure beneath our metrically oriented notation. After all, the situation he is trying to deal with is an age-old one. The tension he describes—roughly that between metric and rhythmic organization—is only one aspect of the tension between conception and notation, and the conse-quent tension between notation and performance. He is trying to codify and record distinctions that are too subtle for the conven-tional system of notation—and perhaps for any system. But that does not mean that composers and performers have been insensitive to the relevant distinctions. They are embedded in the rhythmic structure of each composition and are made manifest by the articulations, phrasings, and rubati of its performances. If composers today still seem to ignore these elements in their scores and in their discussions of the music that interests them, it is not necessarily because they are either ignorant or scornful of such matters: like the composers of the past, they may prefer to rely on the musical wisdom of the performer (or the analyst) to supply, in actuality or in imagination, inflections too subtle to be recorded on paper.

Of course one should strive for the greatest possible accuracy of notation; but one should remember that the operative word here is "possible." Absolute accuracy, except in certain limited areas (indicated pitches on the piano, for example), is out of the question. Most notation merely limits the range of choices open to the performer (a passing chromatic G♯ on the violin must lie somewhere between a presumably established G and A, and probably not closer to G than to A). From this point of view, "indeterminate notation," which exaggerates the performer's freedom of choice, is a useful reminder of the relativity of all notation.

Electronic music of the recorded kind must, by nature, get along without the possibility of such variation in performance; indeed, it represents, in an odd way, the ideal of absolutely accurate notation. For some composers this is a prime advantage of the medium: they would recast the above sentence to read, "Electronic music . . . is uniquely privileged to get along without the possibility of such variation in performance." But this privilege entails an obvious responsibility: the composer must perform—must uniquely perform—his own work. As a result, he must give it the kind of study required to enable him to "play" it effectively —or, to approach the problem from another point of view, he must "notate" it with the accuracy afforded and demanded by the medium, an accuracy that can and must be applied to nuances of articulation that have hitherto perforce been left to the individual performer. Specifically, the composer must attempt to "interpret" metrical events in rhythmic terms in such a way as to avoid an electronic analogue of the square and inflexible performances that Riemann deplored. The difficulty is intrinsic but by no means insuperable. The best electronic productions demonstrate that it is not; in them, composition, notation, and performance become uniquely one.

B. A. B.
E. T. C.

CONTENTS

AMERICAN PERFORMANCE AND
NEW MUSIC

GUNTHER SCHULLER

————————————■▪▪▪▪▪■————————————

In a country as vast as ours, it is well-nigh impossible for any individual to assess standards of musical performance accurately, even as they bear upon an area so specialized as contemporary music. Musical activity takes place in such a large number of localities, is practiced by such a variety of organizations and on so many different planes, that one could probably make the available statistical data support any theory one wished to promulgate. In this welter of activity, however, one fact seems to stand out: the mean level of American performance standards has risen considerably in the last two decades at a rate that is proportionately higher than anywhere else in the world. Though the American composer may not always realize or appreciate it, he is the beneficiary of this widening spiral of improvement which applies to all styles and degrees of contemporaneity and is informed and nurtured by the specific characteristics of our competitive social system.

This is not to say that there is no room for improvement on the part of performers, nor that performers have solved the practical problems occasioned by the greatly increased demands of today's music. But if we consider that Western musical tradition has undergone two rather drastic "revolutions" in our century (one in the first two decades and the other within the last fifteen years), the extent to which our musicians have been able to keep abreast of these rampaging developments is rather surprising.

Statistics relating to the performance of "contemporary music" such as those published by the American Symphony Orchestra League reveal that the greater part of this repertory is not "contemporary" in any sense that this much-abused term is understood in this journal. In such lists, anything composed in the twentieth century—even works such as Stravinsky's *Firebird*, and early Bartók and Prokofieff—are classed as "contemporary."

Obviously, statistics based on such premises are misleading and meaningless. Thus, within the context of this article, performance problems will be discussed in terms of that "contemporary music" which deals with techniques and concepts evolved in the last two decades, or with other aspects not yet assimilated into the mainstream of American performance practices—the music, in other words, which is often erroneously called "experimental" or "avant-garde."

While I am sometimes astounded at the excellence of performances of "advanced" music, especially (and most frequently) in the hands of the youngest generation of musicians, I am at other times left with the impression that too many performers, regardless of their technical competence, are totally unaware of the new problems that have been brought to the fore by recent compositional developments. This is even true—in fact perhaps most often true—of our technically best equipped professionals, who may have sufficient instrumental skill to play an advanced contemporary work immaculately from a mechanical point of view, but who often lack any rapport with the new concepts that may have inspired it.

All too often, conductors and instrumentalists still search for traditional harmonic functions, and are unable to accept the principle of intervallic autonomy found in most recent music. They are even less aware of the new roles played by such elements as dynamics and timbre, which have been accorded structural functions that can no longer be realized by means of the subjective, approximate approach of nineteenth-century interpretational mannerisms. (This, however, does not rule out the fact that in time a whole new set of "instinctive" performance practices, expressive of newer musical concepts, may be developed.) After nearly two centuries of this attitude, composers may have to exercise considerable patience until newer concepts are assimilated, and the technical instrumental problems created thereby solved. Perhaps the first requirement for the realization of these goals is the recognition that new performance demands do not necessarily imply the discarding of that older criteria. It is not so much a matter of renouncing the old, although this is sometimes also necessary, as of extending and enriching our musical language by accepting the new. As Varèse once put it: "Just because there are other ways of getting there, you do not kill the horse."

The point-to-point continuity of contemporary music also remains largely misunderstood by performers. It is, of course, often simply rejected as the "aberration" of a "mathematically inclined" generation of composers. But even at a more sophisticated level, conductors and performers who have accepted the new formal and structural concepts as a *fait accompli*, often do not know how to bring them off. Consider, for example, the average musician's inability to cope with just two of the ideas most prevalent in today's new music: various uses of *Klang-farbenmelodie* and its extension into pointillism. In both, the single performer's previous role as an *individualistic* carrier of the melodic-expressive component is transformed into a *communal* one. The player no longer bears an entire melodic burden, but is asked to share it in specific ways with other instruments and players. Tone-color melody, in its most orthodox sense as a kind of "melodic dovetailing" distributed among several instruments, requires a degree of attack-and-release precision and timbral control that most players are totally unprepared for. To the player, the very idea that he is given only one note in a chain of melodic segments seems to be an affront to his carefully built-up, ego-nurtured sense of importance. It need hardly be emphasized that distortions in phrasing that are perpetrated in the name of "musical expression" are offensive enough in older music; but in a music predicated on a totally different kind of "expressive" content they are simply incongruous and absurd.

Some progress has been made in the realm of "attack" (or "touch") control, necessitated by the new structural and textural functions of this factor. However, the manner of release is undoubtedly the most neglected and abused aspect of instrumental control. Whereas the romantic era taught us to taper notes gracefully, to mould them personally, and allowed for a certain degree of freedom in their release, contemporary forms of expression often require a degree of precision and bowing or breath control that approximates the very precise conditions of electronic music. This specific problem is very much related to the entire question of rhythmic accuracy, today's primary performance problem, which is discussed below. In "pointillistic" procedures, the instrumentalist's perplexities are compounded. Not only must he worry about the exact, often fractionalized duration of the note in question, but he must learn to play short notes with a refinement of sonority never before specified. Mostly as a result of misunderstanding, pointillistic or greatly fragmented structures often sound like a series of uncontrolled bleats and grunts. It has never occurred to some players that an isolated staccato note need not be choked off or blatant in its sonority (and consequently be unintentionally humorous). Both wind and string players would do well to learn that a short note is simply a shorter version of what could just as well have been a long note! The point is that the care in attack and tone control expended on a long note is equally required for a staccato note, if it is to form a meaningful moment within a larger continuity.

Questions of style in contemporary music also remain largely unresolved. While it is perhaps too early to expect stylistic differentiations in performances of the most recent works, it is precisely such qualities which make a composition memorable, and performers must quickly learn to direct their attention to them. Performances that capture this stylistic quintessence can do more to transmit an understanding of a new work than a merely pedantic rendering of its structural skeleton. In saying this I am not advocating a return to the "expressive" excesses of earlier periods, but simply remarking the necessity to strike a balance between the mechanical-technical aspects and the musical— the expressive—elements. Most often the latter can, of course, be deduced from the former, and in the case of the especially prescient musician, even intuitively felt. However, this link between the mechanical details of a composition and that which emerges between the lines, so to speak, in actual performance, is very rarely experienced in contemporary music; one tries in vain to call to memory more than a handful of performances that revealed the beauty and essence of the best of today's music. Similarly, one can think of a number of influential recordings of important contemporary works incorporating stylistic distortion (despite a degree of mechanical accuracy) whose effect will take many years to rectify.

I have already suggested that the most urgent problems in contemporary music relate to rhythm. Not only has the variety of available rhythmic patterns increased manifoldly in our century, but the new degree of rhythmic-polyphonic independence requires a kind of accuracy for which the traditional limited repertory of simple divisive patterns leave us ill-prepared. If one were to test a group of musicians of all levels of professionalism, with one extremely elementary rhythmic exercise, namely the playing of a moderately slow three against two, the percentage of accurate readings would be shockingly low. If we have not yet learned how to play a precise triplet, what then can we do with today's quintuplets, septuplets and other even more complex "irrational" rhythmic constellations.

But the performer is not alone in facing the challenge presented by newly acquired rhythmic possibilities. The composer has certain responsibilities too. Some new music abounds in rhythmic configurations that are literally unplayable. Whereas a few years ago composers were still legitimately involved in exploring new rhythmic possibilities, I doubt that any further *reasonable* rhythmic figures can be discovered, and it seems to me that composers today should concentrate on finding those complex or "irrational" rhythms that can be incorporated into a practical repertoire. If a composer must go beyond the point already reached, he is well advised to compose for electronic media. Many composers in their fascination with new rhythmic concepts seem to have "intellectualized" these beyond all performance realities; this is not less true because one or two inordinately gifted musicians (read: pianists) can approximate with a semblance of accuracy some of the still more involved rhythmic structures appearing in today's music. In ensembles or orchestras, such structures are merely absurd. Even if a passage such as the following example (hypothetical, but similar to existing ones)

Ex. 1

could be played accurately,[1] there are several more logical and practical notations possible. And beyond that, it is hardly likely that a conversion into:

Ex. 2

would result in a difference so vital that the loss in "serial" pedigree would not be more than outweighed by the increased playability of the passage. For any serial operations which have not been aurally-mentally and perhaps concretely tested by the composer are an aesthetic absurdity, and are bound to fail in terms of performance realities (at

[1] In Ex. 1 the first 32nd notes have a duration of 8/35 of a second per note; the remaining eleven, 12/55. Reduced to a more easily apprehensible approximation, the relationship of the two rhythmic patterns on a per-note basis is 4/17 to 4/18. I defy anyone to differentiate the two speeds accurately and with certainty in performance. Similarly, I find it impossible to believe that a musician could accurately compress five beats (or units) into the time of four, while *simultaneously* protracting two subdivisions thereof in two dissimilar segments, and both at different rates of protraction. The best that such a passage deserves is what it usually gets, an educated guess. (Ex. 1 is admittedly an extreme but by no means unrepresentative case.)

least of the "human" kind). It is one thing to sit for hours at a desk and devise the most complex rhythmic configurations that are notationally possible. It is entirely different to have to play them in split seconds.

I trust that these remarks will not be equated with musical reaction. Undoubtedly great strides will still be made toward enlarging the scope of rhythmic capabilities. But I would hazard the prediction that any such advances will be in the realm of increased sensitivity and accuracy and, to judge from past history as well as from the spectacular developments in jazz (where tempos of $\mathsf{J} = 340$ are by no means rare), in our ability to perceive rhythmic events passing by at much greater velocities. It is already demonstrable that the beat—in so far as it exists as such in contemporary music—is perceived at an increasingly faster rate, and our sense of the microcosmic structure of time divisions has been greatly developed in recent years. I seriously doubt, however, that the human ear can *accurately* translate into physical impulses that which is in the first instance determined only by arithmetic calculations (as in Ex. 1) or by notational mannerisms which actually represent ideas essentially external to music itself. For rhythms must ultimately be *felt* if they are ever to be played accurately. As far as *performance* goes they simply cannot remain at the level of intellectual apprehension, but must be translated into physical impulses. Reflexes can, of course, be trained to react to more complex impulses, but within each generation or each historical period there seem to be certain limits in this respect; at the very least, it takes a certain amount of time to acquire such new reflexive habits.

Many composers recognize that, with the recently developed extremes of complexity, we have also reached an impasse between notation and realization. They have therefore adopted new means of notation, which some have coupled with improvisational or "indeterminate" techniques that circumvent rhythmic problems in the above sense altogether. Aside from the aesthetic question involved in such concepts, they do not solve the "rhythmic" issue either, but simply evade it.

While rhythmic problems involve both performers and composers, questions of dynamics lie mainly in the hands of performers. Here again, there is a long-held tradition of bad habits, such as the ignoring of dynamics in all but the final stages of rehearsal, the absence of any precise definition of loudness degrees, and a general failure to understand their function. With today's tendency to abstract dynamics and give them a more functional role, their imprecise rendering is no longer merely a matter of carelessness or poor interpretation; now it subverts and annuls a vital structural element, in terms of which one no longer can speak of a "poor" performance, but rather of a "wrong" one. If the admonition of certain great musicians to "read the dynamics first" was sound advice in the past, it has become an essential today.

Another facet of the "dynamic" problem is the new way that sudden dynamic changes are used. At one time these were almost entirely a means of achieving contrast and "expressive" surprises. But today they also function as a means to delineate the internal design of polyphonic structures and larger formal schemes. The frequent use of highly differentiated dynamic levels not only requires maximum technical control of the instrument, but also a much increased mental agility. It would be difficult to say whether the musicians' inability to play a sequence of notes which has a different ungraduated dynamic for each note (our hypothetical example can again serve to illustrate an extreme case) stems more from lack of training or sheer resentment of such a passage. In either case, a re-evaluation of the functionality of dynamics in today's music (at least as a concept) is long overdue, especially since it would uncover the new-found beauty of dynamics used as a pure musical element that need not necessarily play a secondary role.

In the orchestra all these problems are aggravated, especially the rhythmic ones. Conductors—insofar as they are not themselves delinquent—spend the greater part of their rehearsal time correcting poorly read rhythms. Aside from the newness of the problem and the actual technical difficulties involved, there is one other fundamental reason for this dilatoriness, one peculiar to the United States. As a musical culture we are not only still young, but also not yet homogenous. That is to say, the individual traits of the different nationalities that make up our orchestras still persist. A musician with an Italian background "feels" rhythms quite differently from one with a German training. At this stage of our musical acculturation, the varied European influences are still to a large extent operative, and as a result very few orchestras can boast of a uniform rhythmic conception. Obviously a slight divergence at the most elementary rhythmic levels is bound to increase with complex patterns. The extent to which the composer should take this factor into account is, I suppose, entirely dependent on his own musical attitudes. There are a few notable exceptions to this limitation, for example the Chicago and Cleveland Orchestras, which are in certain crucial respects the finest orchestras in America, having been trained by two of the world's foremost orchestral disciplinarians. It is therefore especially lamentable that they are very rarely given the opportunity to play any really contemporary music.

The conglomerate complexion of our orchestras has its good side too. Even the poorest American instrumental group plays with a natural rhythmic vitality and drive quite unknown in Europe. The discipline of a good German orchestra is achieved at the expense of rhythmic drive and a kind of propulsive inner energy; their performances tend to be vertically accurate, but horizontally phlegmatic. No doubt this splendid characteristic of our American instrumentalists is an unintentional side-effect of the vitality of our popular cultures, particularly jazz. It also explains to some extent why much of the best American contemporary music is received with such indifference in Europe; when played by European orchestras, its innate characteristic vitality and virtuosity cannot be properly realized.

Improvement of this situation can only come if our educational institutions develop a closer awareness of the musical realities of our time. I think it was Mark Twain who said that we must cling to only that part of the past which can be of value to us in the present and the future. Considering the musical potential of this country, it is sad to think that we are best at producing pianists who win competitions in other lands playing Tchaikovsky and Rachmaninoff. Our genius and great talent may survive, but ultimately even they need the foundation and background of a culture which remains vital and in contact with the present, if they are to flourish.

1963

PROBLEMS AND
METHODS OF NOTATION

KURT STONE

TODAY, in that area of our newest music which claims Webern as its founder, most of the basic forces that hitherto served to create musical logic and coherence have lost their a priori position of supremacy; now elements that had been of secondary importance, or had not even been considered part of music, have become the shaping factors of a new musical language.

The chief trends of this development run in two very different directions: 1) toward uncompromising exactitude and predictability; 2) toward chance. The present article constitutes a broad outline of new notational problems raised by "controlled music" and a sampling of notational innovations designed to solve them. It is further limited to discussing published works or works about to be published so that readers may have access to scores.

Compared to the iconoclastic efforts of the "chance musicians," the notational innovations of "controlled" composers look unspectacular for the most part. Yet, the notational dilemma in which these composers find themselves is much greater than that which confronts their "aleatory" colleagues. Today's composers of predetermined music cannot permit themselves to leave anything to chance. All aspects of their music are more meticulously calculated than ever before and must be conveyed to the performer with unprecedented notational exactitude. Traditional notation simply cannot always cope satisfactorily with such demands. One merely needs to consider the inordinate amount of rehearsal time which is required to achieve a reasonably accurate interpretation of a complex score to realize why relaxed and intelligent performances have become such a rarity.

Four aspects of a musical composition which must be expressed (by means of the directional signs of notation) with sufficient explicitness to enable the performer properly to interpret the composer's intentions are pitch, tempo, rhythm (and meter), and articulation.

PITCH

In this domain, conventional notation was able to reflect, through proper chromatic spelling, the subtlest inner harmonic workings of music of the tonal era. This established system of notation lends itself to even more sensitive pitch specification than our well-tempered instruments can reproduce. In the harmonic language of extended chromatic functionalism (Debussy, Hindemith, etc.) a considerable degree of "logical" spelling was still possible, though discrepancies between music and notation became increasingly apparent. As soon as the twelve tones are treated as equal, independent pitch elements, however, the availability of four different "accidentals" ($\sharp$, $\times$, $\flat$, $\flat\flat$), and of three different spellings for most pitches (D$\sharp$, E$\flat$, F$\flat\flat$)—indeed, that we have accidentals at all—becomes irrelevant. In much of today's music the traditional system of accidentals is no longer the tool of harmonic precision that it once was; instead it has become an often misleading encumbrance. The obvious visual symptom of this is the profusion of mnemonic parenthetical accidentals found in modern scores, as well as the frequent practice of placing a natural or accidental in front of every note (so that the performer must always read two signs, instead of one).

And yet, composers have done little about this problem, no doubt because the traditional system of accidentals, no matter how incongruous its original rationale has become in our new musical context, can at least serve the necessary purpose. So long as it does, it is probably unlikely that anyone will succeed in convincing busy professional musicians of the necessity, let alone desirability, of learning a brand new system of notation.

One such system that was recently proposed might, however, be worth touching upon, since it differs in an important aspect from most other accidental-free pitch notations: instead of increasing the number of staff lines, it reduces them to one per octave. This system, called "Equiton," was developed by Erhard Karkoschka[1] after having been proposed originally (according to Karkoschka) by Rodney Fawcett in 1958. In "Equiton" notation, a chromatic scale from C_3 through C_4 would look as follows:

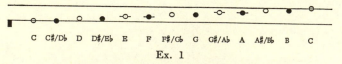

| C | C$\sharp$/D$\flat$ | D | D$\sharp$/E$\flat$ | E | F | F$\sharp$/G$\flat$ | G | G$\sharp$/A$\flat$ | A | A$\sharp$/B$\flat$ | B | C |

Ex. 1

The reader would have to become used to perceiving, without the aid of staff lines, whether E and F or G$\sharp$/A$\flat$ and A are closer to the upper or lower C-line. The notes F$\sharp$/G$\flat$ and G present no problem since no other such notes appear in mid-space between the C-lines.

[1] Erhard Karkoschka, "Ich habe mit Equiton komponiert," *Melos*, VII/VIII (Mainz, 1962), pp. 232-239.

Chords can be written either:

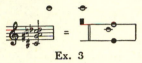

Ex. 2

or, in the case of minor seconds, by combining a white and a black note in a single note-symbol:

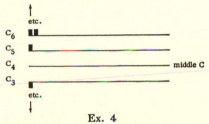

Ex. 3

At the beginning of the C-line, a "clef" indicates which C the line represents:

Ex. 4

Durations are expressed by proportionate horizontal spacing of the notes and by extension lines. Bar lines, dotted bar lines, and short vertical strokes for metric subdivisions may be added. Two short slanted strokes are used for whole bar rests; all other rests are expressed by one single sign (⅄) which simply remains effective until the next note or bar line.

In polyphonic textures, the extension lines can be used to indicate voice crossings in addition to durations:

Ex. 5

"Equiton" does not yet include a new pitch nomenclature although it provides twelve *individual* pitch symbols instead of the customary seven "white" notes and their chromatic modifications.

To repeat: it is most improbable that new pitch notations would be really practical at the present time. Should, however, the division of the octave into more than twelve pitch elements become sufficiently important to composers, the question of whether to adapt conventional staff notation or to invent a new notation such as "Equiton" will become much more pressing.

At present, only a few incidental or ornamental deviations from the conventional twelve-tone division are in use. These are, of course, not at all structural and are usually dealt with quite adequately by means of a few simple and obvious signs: a small arrow above or next to a note or accidental, or an arrowhead directly connected to an accidental, such as in Mauricio Kagel's *Sexteto de cuerdas* (1953/57):[2]

Ex. 6

Schoenberg, in his *Harmonielehre*, predicted that the tempered twelve-tone scale would soon have to be superseded by others since its tuning and structure constitute a mere "truce" rather than a real solution of the acoustical problems involved. Besides, throughout history new octave divisions have been proposed. Some of the more recent ones are of special interest here. Adriaan D. Fokker,[3] for example, outlines a division into 31 steps, reviving, he says, a theory first developed 300 years ago by Christiaan Huygens (1629-1695). The interval of a whole tone would, in this scale, be divided into five steps which would be notated partly by means of conventional accidentals, partly with accidentals proposed by Giuseppe Tartini (in 1756), and partly with Fokker's (and Henk Badings') adaptations. This would make possible the retention of the five-line staff:

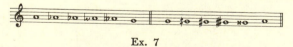

Ex. 7

Since, however, neither Fokker's octave division nor any of the others (such as Harry Partch's 43-tone octave or Joseph Yasser's

---

[2] At first occurrence of each work, the date(s) of composition is given. When no such date could be ascertained, the copyright date appears, identified by a ©.

[3] Adriaan D. Fokker, "Wozu und warum? Fragen zur neuen Musik," *Die Reihe*, VIII (Vienna, 1962), pp. 70-72, and "Genauere Bestimmung der Tonhöhe," *Musica*, XVI, 1 (Kassel, 1962), p. 37.

"supra-diatonic" 19-tone scale, to mention two American efforts) has as yet won wide acceptance, a more detailed discussion here of their notational implications would be premature.

TEMPO

Tempo, steadily maintained, presents relatively few notational problems. Regular rates of speed continue to be specified by metronome marks (although there are exceptions, as will be seen below). Gradual changes of speed, however, are more difficult to notate if greater precision is desired than can be conveyed by the traditional directions rit. and accel. and their vague modifiers *poco*, *molto*, etc.

The speed-change symbol most frequently encountered in modern scores is the long slanted line terminated at the right in an arrowhead. Changes from one specific speed to another are sometimes indicated by way of added metronome numbers or by degree numbers on a scale of relative speeds, as in Pierre Boulez' *Improvisation sur Mallarmé— Une dentelle s'abolit* (© 1958):

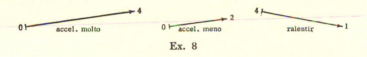

Ex. 8

(In the latter method, there is usually a key which indicates the exact metronomic equivalent for some or all of the speed-scale numbers, "0" being the *tempo giusto* of the piece or section.) Sometimes the rate of acceleration or deceleration is not to be constant. This can be indicated by angled or curved lines:

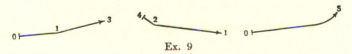

Ex. 9

Adaptations of the slanting arrows are found too. In such cases the arrows may run through the beams of a group of notes, indicating a momentary speeding up or slowing down of the grouplet so marked— a controlled rubato (if such a paradoxical concept is admissible):

Ex. 10

Less novel but much more explicit is the method used by Elliott Carter in his more recent scores. Instead of only indicating initial and terminal speeds, he adds metronomic indications throughout the course of extended ritardandi or accelerandi. Although many of these intervening numbers do not actually appear on existing metronomic instruments, they convey to the player the rate at which the speed is to change (see Ex. 11).

Carter usually spells out shorter phrases of gradually changing speeds by means of increasing or decreasing note values. This method becomes imperative where not all parts participate in the speed change or where they increase or decrease at different rates.

Some composers make the tempos of their compositions dependent on specific circumstances and rules which differ from piece to piece or from performance to performance. Although such systems do not fall within the area of notation as it concerns us here because they lack universal applicability, a few such instances might be mentioned.

In Bo Nilsson's *Quantitäten* for piano (© 1958), the notated time values are modified by the pitches of the notes involved. According to the instructions, each note value may have any of 85 durations, since the piece contains 85 different pitches.

In Karlheinz Stockhausen's *Zeitmasse* for five woodwinds (1957), the greatest speed at which the performers can play the shortest notes determines the fastest tempo of a group, and the longest period of time the players can hold their longest notes determines the slowest tempos. All speed changes are in the proportion 4:1 or 1:4, and the length of each group determines the rate at which the tempo changes.

Sometimes tempos are indicated in seconds-per-page or per line, as in John Cage's *Music for Carillon I* (1952/61) or Earle Brown's *Music for Cello and Piano* (1955) and *Hodograph I* (1959). In most

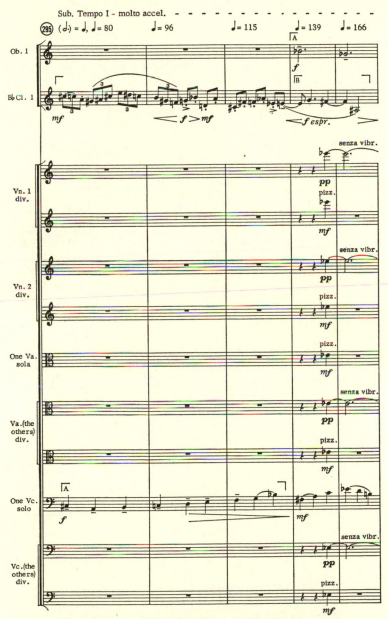

Ex. 11. Elliott Carter: *Variations for Orchestra* (1954/55)

other respects, however, compositions of this kind generally do not fall within the area of controlled music.

Since much contemporary music operates with carefully planned silences between sounds, long rests are often replaced by square fermatas; and these, in turn, occasionally appear in combination with numerals indicating the number of seconds the silences are to last. Sometimes such numbered square fermatas are also used to indicate the number of seconds a tone is to be held:

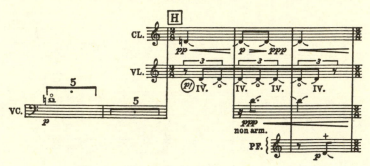

Ex. 12. Niccolò Castiglioni: *Tropi* (1959)

In this example the first cello D is to be held for five seconds and is to be followed by a five-second rest.

Another use of square fermatas is to signify the suspension of all controlled rhythm, etc., usually for an unspecified duration (Boulez' *Improvisation—Une dentelle . . .* , p. 24).

RHYTHM

No other aspect of contemporary notation is more desperately in need of fundamental revision than that of rhythm. Most of today's rhythmic structures are far more complex—as well as rigid, or, conversely, free and flexible—than the pulse-generated and pulse-dominated rhythms of the past. Conventional notation always presupposes pulse; it knows only regularities and irregularities of metric pulse. It does not provide adequate means for the precise notation of pulseless, a-metrical rhythmic structures or of controlled ritardandi and accelerandi.

Conventional notation is, in addition, severely limited by its bipartite system of note values, a system which operates with only one single geometric progression for all primary durations: 2, 4, 8, 16, etc. As soon as a rhythm deviates from these simple divisions and multiples, as soon as a division merely becomes tripartite, one must resort to makeshift devices such as prolongation dots and/or ties. Should the rhythm go but one step further from the norm, even in the simplest traditional music, then brackets with small numerals are needed to denote duplets in triple time, triplets in duple time, quadruplets, quintuplets, and so forth, and before long the modifying signs and symbols—dots, ties, brackets, and numerals, lengthened or shortened additionally by fermatas, tenuto lines, staccato dots, phrasing slurs, breath marks, etc.—far outnumber the actual notes.

One of the first composers to recognize this dilemma, and possibly the very first to attempt a practical solution, was Henry Cowell who, in 1917, notated his piano piece *Fabric*[4] with an expanded system of note values. Here the whole note, in addition to its conventional bipartite divisions, is also divisible by 3, 5, 7, 9, 11, 13, and 15, and each such division is subdivided according to the usual geometric progression. The new values are symbolized by note-heads whose outward appearance was inspired by the old American shape notes. Thus, half-note triplets become 3rd-notes: ♩ ♩ ♩ , etc.

For example:

2/3rds-note = ▵	4/5ths-note = ▢
3rd-note = ♩	2/5ths-note = ◻
6th-note = ♪	5th-note = ◗
12th-note = ♪	10th-note = ◗
etc.	etc.

Although Cowell retained prolongation dots and ties, he made unnecessary the use of brackets and numerals denoting compound groups. An example in the explanatory introduction to the piece shows how the system works:

Ex. 13

Unfortunately, because of the essentially simple nature of *Fabric*, many problems remain unsolved. For example, the piece contains no chords in close position and only three kinds of rests: an ordinary 8th-rest, a 12th-rest (the bottom having the triangular shape of the

4 Published with detailed explanations in 1922 by Breitkopf Publications, Inc., New York, and included in the collection "Piano Music by Henry Cowell," issued in 1961 by Associated Music Publishers, Inc., New York.

2/3rds-note and its family), and a 14th-rest (incorporating the diamond shape of the 4/7ths-note and its family).

This system has remained an oddity—no one, not even Cowell himself, has made further use of it. Besides, it still assumes motion in terms of regular metric pulse beats while much of our present music does not.

A single page of the score of Carter's String Quartet No. 2 (1959) will serve to demonstrate the present rhythmic dilemma:

Ex. 14

In the first measure and a half, regular beats move at slightly different rates of speed. Were it not for the fact that the different metric pulses must be played in precise rhythmic relation to each other, the cello, and similarly the viola and the second violin, could be notated in the following way to convey a rhythm (at least in a short phrase) which the player could grasp at a glance:

Of course, the work cannot be notated in this way throughout—only a few isolated spots lend themselves to it—but in a simpler composition of similar style, i.e. one that also operates with different pulses, such notation could be imagined. Each instrument would then have to have its own metronomic speed and its own time signature (if it is considered necessary to have one at all). In this way, the notational images of the different metric components would come very much closer to the musical phenomena they are meant to represent than notation governed by a general metric denominator. Unfortunately, ensemble playing from such parts would be virtually impossible.

In the middle of the second measure, beginning with the high A in the cello, the predicament becomes even greater: while the violins continue at regular pulse, the cello now has an accelerando followed by a ritardando. (The viola does not have any real metric pulse at all here.) This time a simplified cello notation such as

Ex. 15

could not even be programmed for performance by synthesizer because the notes do not show the slight difference in the *rate* at which the speed increases and decreases. On the other hand, Carter's own notation is also unsatisfactory, because it is incapable of conveying the

smoothness of speed change which he himself wants in this passage.
It is for this reason that he added the dotted slur which is intended
to make the successive note values flow more evenly than notated. In
passages slurred in this way, only the first and last notes, respectively,
are to be played at their notated values. The intervening notes are to
be played quite freely; their notated durations only indicate whether
the gradual speed change is regular or more active at the beginning
or at the end of the passage.[5] In the above example the rate of activity
progresses as follows (taking the value of a 32nd-note as the basic
unit: 32nd-note $= 1$):

Ex. 16

It may be illuminating to apply some of the methods most frequently proposed for dealing with this notational problem to the above
passage from Carter's quartet. These methods are all variations of
what is commonly referred to as "proportionate notation."

1) Conventional notation, spaced horizontally in geometrically
exact equivalents of rhythmic proportions:

Ex. 17

In spite of certain advantages, this method constitutes only a partial
solution of the problem, since the many, confusing, different note
values, dots, and ties, have all been retained. Proportionate *spacing*
alone does not suffice, at least not when confronted with the com-

[5] See preface of the score.

plexities of contemporary music.[6] Even so, this system has been utilized in Stockhausen's *Zeitmasse*, Cage's *Music of Changes* (1951), and other contemporary scores. Cage even supplies scales based on 2½ cm. = ♩ (or so, at least, he claims):

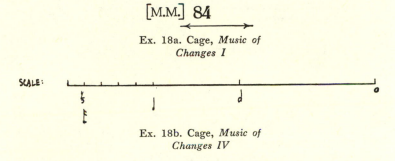

Ex. 18a. Cage, *Music of
Changes I*

Ex. 18b. Cage, *Music of
Changes IV*

2) "Time notation" which has been developed by Earle Browne:

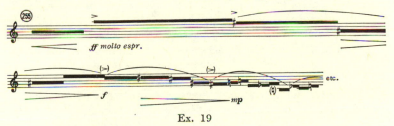

Ex. 19

This method, as illustrated above, replaces the profusion of conventional note values with single "notes" which, through their various lengths (from mere dots to long bars), constitute geometric rather than symbolic representations of durations. Apart from thus providing an unrestricted range of clearly visible durations, the system also has other advantages. For example, legato slurs, staccato dots, and many other related signs of articulation become superfluous because the length of the pitch indicators and their positions relative to each other (detached, overlapping, etc.) take their place. On the other hand, exact placement of the pitch indicators is sometimes hampered because of the space required for accidentals. (For example, the A and G♯ at the beginning cannot be as closely connected as, say, the subsequent A♯ and E, because of the intervening sharps.)

[6] It has been very helpful in the presentation of older music, as exemplified in M. van Crevel's edition of the *Missa Sub Tuum Presidium* by Jacob Obrecht, issued by the Vereniging voor Nederlandse Muziekgeschiedenis (Amsterdam, 1959/60).

3) Proportionate notation which uses traditional, stemmed, black note heads as pitch indicators, and beams of varying lengths as duration indicators:

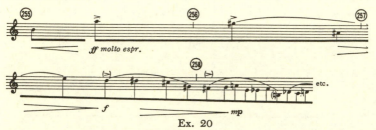

Ex. 20

In this method (often identified with Luciano Berio),[7] proportionate spacing of the notes conveys their rhythmic position within the context of the composition, and beams indicate their durations. In addition, short, equidistant tactus strokes, their speed governed by metronome marks, indicate a regular pulsation. This pulsation need not necessarily coincide with the pulse of the music itself; if the music is without pulse or if its pulse keeps changing or is different in different parts, the strokes function as a musically neutral framework.

The "Equiton" notation mentioned earlier, aims in the same direction: it too combines proportionate spacing, durational extension lines, and bar lines (tacti). It even includes subsidiary bar lines, a "crutch" upon which some composers who use conventional notation have also leaned. Incidentally, a surprisingly illogical flaw of many proportionate notational systems, including "Equiton," is the placing of the bar line in its conventional position, i.e. *before* the actual beat.

In spite of the methods discussed, it must be concluded that conventional notation, no matter how cumbersome and alien it is as a graphic vehicle for today's music, is still the only method which ensures that the performer will be able to reproduce exactly what he sees. Even the addition of tactus strokes to proportionate notation (using nonsymbolic notes) is of only limited value in this respect, considering the rhythmic complexities of today's music. Human beings simply do not seem to possess a space perception equal in acuity to their pulse perception; if they are not given something they can count, they will not be able to play "in time." Even the counting of a neutral tactus, i.e. a pulse unrelated to the actual meter or rhythm, is extremely difficult if the notes themselves do not symbolize countable time values.

On a far more utilitarian level, proportionate notation poses another problem: page turns in instrumental parts. Regardless of how crowded

[7] See for example his *Sequenza* for solo flute (1958).

or open the conventionally notated part page is, the rhythmic explicitness of the music remains unaffected. This remarkable horizontal flexibility is indispensable for making good page turns possible. Proportionate notation lacks this flexibility. Furthermore, if nonsymbolic notes are used, a performer can only play in time with other performers as long as he sees his own notes in spatial relation to theirs. This means that an individual part, all by itself, cannot be used; each part *must* show the other parts, or at least their prominent rhythmic features. In music for small ensemble this presents no great problem. Each player can be provided with a full score and if need be a page turner. But for larger ensembles a full score (not to mention the page turners!) would take up too much space. In such cases a continuous cue line containing a reduction of the total score must be printed above or below the actual part in order to ensure reasonably accurate ensemble playing.

The value of such cue lines was recognized years ago, and some conventionally notated parts of unusually complex works contain them. See, for instance, the parts of Berg's String Quartet (1910), both String Quartets by Carter, or the Second String Quartet (1958) by Leon Kirchner.

Since conventional notation must, in most cases, be used for lack of a better method, a good many practices (some of which might be called relief measures) have been developed in recent years. The continuous cue line is one; another is the use of extended beams (and extended brackets for compound grouplets) to clarify *metric* counting units, regardless of the *rhythmic* groupings of the notes. Another Carter example,[8] notated two ways, shows what is meant:

Ex. 21

[8] *Double Concerto for Harpsichord and Piano with Two Chamber Orchestras* (1961).

Ex. 22

Needless to say, the rhythms proceed independently of each other and of the meter. Yet, the meter governs the beaming in order to be as effective as possible in its role as neutral coordinator. (This is of course a comparatively simple case because, unlike the earlier Carter example, all parts fit a common metric denominator.)

Another helpful innovation is the addition of clarifying notes or numbers to the small compound numerals. As yet there is little uniformity; a few different approaches follow:

Ex. 23. Pierre Boulez, *Piano Sonata III*
(*formant 2: trope*) (© 1961)

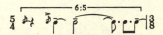

Ex. 24. Roman Haubenstock-Ramati,
Séquences, for violin and
orchestra (1958)

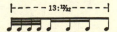

Ex. 25. Franco Evangelisti, *Proiezioni sonore*,
structure for piano solo (1955/56)

Ex. 26. Elliott Carter, *Double Concerto*

(Carter's explicit indications appear only in doubtful cases[9] or at the first occurrence of a certain type of compound grouping.)

As the examples show, only Carter focuses on the entire beat unit; the others concern themselves with details of proportions *within* a unit. Carter and Evangelisti are explicit about the actual note values involved; Boulez and Haubenstock-Ramati leave it to the player to determine what they are. Curiously enough, it is the least explicit method (Haubenstock-Ramati) which is found most frequently. The following from Pousseur's Symphonies for 15 soloists (1954-1955) shows how confusing this method can be:

Ex. 27

Although no notational trick will make this measure easy to play at sight, the Carter methods would at least tell the player that the four 8th beats are divided into three units: ♪ ♪. ♪. , and that 32nd-notes must fit into the first two of these, and 16th notes into the last.

Even though most composers still use conventional notation exclusively, there are important variations in the way they employ it. Thus a composer's attitude toward rhythmic notation, to touch upon the most noticeable variation, often does not depend on musical appropriateness but simply on personal preference. For example, the Carter notation just discussed shows his tendency toward a relatively simple metric framework into which he fits all the many rhythmic complexities and diversities which typify his music. The beaming by beats is utilitarian rather than musical; the musically proper rhythmic group-

---

[9] There is as yet no agreement among composers, editors, etc., as to the proper note-values for compound groups. While ♫=♫♫ finds no objectors, opinions begin to differ at ♫♫=♫♫ or ♪♪ , and some musicians will change note values between ♫♫♫ and ♫♫♫ (Carter among them) while others will not. A perfectly logical set of rules governing compound groups appears in Hindemith's *Elementary Training for Musicians*, but not everybody agrees with it.

ings and their articulation are conveyed to the performers through the profusion of accents, phrasings, dynamics, etc., in Carter's scores.

Composers of the opposite approach like to give visual support to vacillating rhythms and irregular groupings, phrases, and articulation, by means of correspondingly irregular, nonmetric beaming and note values, and by frequent change of time signature. In the following example the flute and second percussion parts of Ex. 22 have been renotated along these lines:

Ex. 28

While such notation often looks musically more "expressive" than that used by Carter and others it is likely to confuse (rhythmically) players as well as conductors because the metric beats are apt to be obscured.

A selection of some notational devices which have or may become standard procedure is shown in Exx. 29-31.

Conducting Aids

1) Indications clarifying irregular subdivisions of measures:

Example 31 is particularly interesting since it shows a combination of conventional rhythmic notation (violin and bass) and proportionate notation (violas and cellos). The flutist is called upon to conduct this particular measure; the conducting signs, unlike those in the Boulez

Ex. 29. Leon Kirchner, Concerto for violin, cello, ten winds, and percussion (1960)

Ex. 31. Luciano Berio, *Tempi concertati* (1958/59)

Ex. 30. Pierre Boulez, *Improvisation sur Mallarmé—Le vierge . . .* , (© 1958)

(Ex. 30), are spaced proportionately. (The sign shaped like an elongated reversed S indicates that the proportionately notated rhythms need only be approximate.)

2) Indications directing the conductor's attention to important entrances:

Ex. 32. 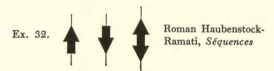 Roman Haubenstock-
Ramati, *Séquences*

Score Setups

Almost all scores of recent vintage are written "in C." (Instrumental parts for transposing instruments are generally but not always issued in the customary transpositions.) In many contemporary scores, measures of rest are simply blanks, without staff lines or bar lines. The chief reasons for this practice are to make the textual image of the music more vivid, and to help the conductor see entrances at a glance.

Dynamics

In all of the following examples, the dynamic levels are built into the notes (thickness equals loudness):

Ex. 33. Berio, *Tempi concertati*

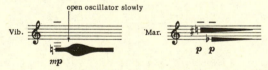

Ex. 34. Brown, *Hodograph I*

Tone Clusters

Perhaps the clearest method of notating tone clusters is that used by Cowell:

Ex. 35

Frequently encountered variations are:

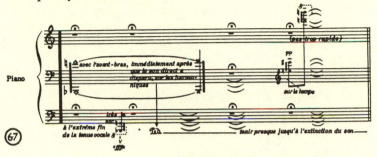

Ex. 36. Boulez, *Improvisation sur Mallarmé—Une Dentelle* . . .

Ex. 37. Evangelisti, *Proiezioni sonore*

Gradual changes of density of a cluster, including the growth from a single tone to a cluster and the reverse, are notated as follows in Krysztof Penderecki's *Threnos* for fifty-two string instruments:

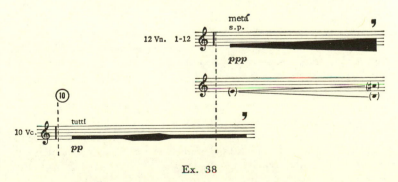

Ex. 38

VOCAL NOTATION

Schoenberg, in *Pierrot Lunaire*, initiated the following note symbols:

♪ = *tonlos* (whispered)   and   ♪ = *Sprechstimme*

Other notations include:

♩ = with closed mouth;   ♩ = with glottal attack

♪ = "approximate pitch (optional: exact pitch)"

Although many additional signs have been developed in recent years (Ralph Shapey has been particularly imaginative in this area), few have as yet become conventions.

The foregoing discussion of the notation of today's "controlled music" raises the questions: what is likely to lie ahead, and is there perhaps a tendency toward reversal of the relative functions of notation and performer.

Notation is a system of directional signs which used to enable a performer conversant with them and with the musical conventions of the era during which they were in use, to recreate a composer's *artistic* vision on the basis of what the *mechanical* directions implied. A listener thus gained ever new insights into a work as it came to life in different performances, colored by the different personalities of the performers.

Some of today's music is constructed in such a way that the slightest modification of *any* of its measurable elements is likely to distort the inner logic of the entire work. In such music, only rigid sign realization is admissible; this music does not permit "interpretation." At the same time, however, music of this nature is generally so complex that truly accurate sign realization is rarely if ever achieved in performance.

Thus, the score and the performer have actually exchanged roles: whereas the score used to be the map designed to guide the performer toward the composer's artistic vision, it now is often completely explicit. On the other hand, performances are now often mere stabs in the direction of the composer's envisioned perfection of execution. The imprecision and variability of human performance are actually quite detrimental to the requirements of totally organized and predetermined works.

Realizing this, composers have begun to relegate such works to electronic performance media which assure absolute accuracy. If this trend becomes a general practice, many of today's notational problems may simply disappear, for almost all of the complexities which are so difficult or even impossible to convey to human performers by means of notational signs can easily be expressed in the programming language of electronic devices. This still leaves unresolved the question of the future of human performances and performers; however, the answer (if there is one) obviously goes far beyond the scope of this discussion.

1963

THE CHANGING COMPOSER-PERFORMER
RELATIONSHIP: A MONOLOGUE
AND A DIALOGUE

LUKAS FOSS

I

ON THE heels of the invaluable discovery of what is commonly referred to as electronic music there followed a diametrically opposed movement endeavoring to draw the performer closer into the composer's laboratory, to build performance at times "into" the composition. This movement consists of a series of efforts in different directions, efforts so full of vague, half-understood implications, that an attempt at objective critical assessment would seem to be premature. Also, I hardly qualify as an objective observer, having been steadily involved with new performance ideas for some time. Thus my remarks here may best be understood as observations made from "within."

Progress in the arts: a series of gifted mistakes perhaps. We owe our greatest musical achievements to an unmusical idea: the division of what is an indivisible whole, "music," into two separate processes: composition (the making of the music) and performance (the making of music), a division as nonsensical as the division of form and content. The history of music is a series of violations, untenable positions, each opening doors, as it were: the well-tempered scale, Wagner's music drama, Stravinsky's neoclassicism, Schoenberg's twelve-tone method, to name but a few. ("My method does not quite work . . . that makes it interesting," Arnold Schoenberg to Gustave Arlt, U.C. L.A.). The methodical division of labor (I write it, you play it) served us well, until composer and performer became like two halves of a worm separated by a knife, each proceeding obliviously on its course.

Around 1915, composition withdrew underground, leaving the field to the performer and to the music of the past. That this created a sterile state of affairs "above" ground was perfectly clear to the more educated virtuoso, who has been trying ever since to resolve the conflict, often leading a Jekyll and Hyde existence on account of it. Thus, Arthur Schnabel gave his audience Beethoven and Schubert; his lifelong involvement with Schoenberg was kept scrupulously to himself. His 1960 counterpart, Glenn Gould, rebels, openly attacks our "narcissistic listening," despises our applause, threatens to retire from the concert circuit at the age of thirty. Leonard Bernstein, deeply aware of the missing element of urgency in our symphonic culture, consoles himself with the musical theater—and so on.

The conflict still rages, and yet the feud between composition and performance is over. The factor which led to the conflict, the division of labor (performance/composition), will remain with us. The procedural advantages are too great to be sacrificed. But a creative investigation is in full swing, and correction of the sterilizing aspects is under way. Composers have had to abandon Beethoven's proud position: "Does he think I have his silly fiddle in mind when the spirit talks to me?" Composers are again involved *in* performance, *with* performance. More—they work with handpicked performers toward a common goal. Among the new composer-performer teams: Cage and Tudor, Boulez and the Südwestfunk, Berio and Cathy Berberian, Babbitt and Bethany Beardslee, Pousseur and a group of seven, my own Improvisation Chamber Ensemble. Each of the teams mentioned is involved in a search, what we might call a joint enterprise in new music. Characteristic here is the composer's fascination with the possibility of new tasks for his new-found partner and confidant. The new tasks demand new ideas of coordination. In fact, the creation of a new vocabulary requires that the composer give constant attention to all performance problems in connection with his score. As a result, a thorough overhauling of conducting technique is in the making, new instrumental discoveries have antiquated every existing orchestration treatise,—traditional limitations of voice and instrument have proved to be mythical: the piano was the first instrument to expand, the flute underwent a change of personality (due largely to Gazzeloni). The human voice followed; percussion came into its own.[1]

The emancipation of percussion and, for that matter, the new use of flute, voice, strings (Penderecki), and *Sprechchor* (Kagel) must actually be attributed to yet another factor: I began by observing that the performance movement directly followed the discovery of electronic music. Paradoxically, it is the advent of electronic music which sparked the performance renaissance.

---

[1] The extent to which percussion has begun to preoccupy the composer can be illustrated by the recent mania for acquiring one's own percussion instruments, then lending them out to percussionists. Stockhausen bought a Degan vibraphone, Berio brought a marimba from San Francisco to Milan, Boulez owns a whole collection of percussion instruments. Can we imagine composers twenty years ago going to such pains to ensure faithful performance?

Electronic music showed up the limitations of live performance, the limitations of traditional tone production, the restrictiveness of a rhythm forever bound to meter and bar line, notation tied to a system of counting. Electronic music introduced untried possibilities, and in so doing presented a challenge, shocked live music out of its inertia, kindled in musicians the desire to prove that live music "can do it too." When I say: "I like my electronic music live," the somewhat flippant remark contains a tribute. Via electronic music came a new approach not only to the above-mentioned instruments and voices, but to their placement on stage, to phonetics, to notation. Percussion found a new climate in a "handmade" white noise. Today, it appears to some that electronic music has served its purpose in thus pointing the way. "Tape fails," says Morton Feldman. And I remember reading in Thomas Mann: "Everything, even nature, turns into mere scenery, background, the instant the human being steps forward."

II

"I beg your pardon if I may be so bold as to interrupt: this new team, this joint 'composer-performer enterprise in new music,' is it to replace the composer's former, solitary work?"

"Give up solitude, and you have given up composition. But performance is always *with* or *for* or both. As to the team (I dislike the word as much as you do), it complements the composer's work, it is a bridge . . ."

"Then all is as it always was, it would seem."

"Yes and no. When I advise a young composer—one so young and foolish as to seek advice—I say: study old and new music, work by yourself. When you grow up, find your performer(s)—and then work by yourself again."

"I am a performer. I am intrigued by the 'laboratory' approach of recent music, but I must admit that I find my powers as an instrumentalist, the capabilities of my instrument, more often abused than used. Playing behind the bridge, inside the piano, slapping the wood, this is not a new task, it is withdrawal to mere marginal possibilities."

"Marginal possibilities are good for marginal purposes . . ."

"And as to the new freedoms and choices suddenly handed to the performer, they seem intriguing and dangerous at first, but soon reveal an inane foolproofness. They are safe, either because the given entities control the desired result, neutralizing my own additions, or because the result does not concern the composer (only the "situation" does). In either instance, I am given choice because 'it matters not what I do.' "

"And that you resent, understandably. But performer-choices where it matters can be accomplished only after years of study. My colleagues of the Improvisation Ensemble and I undertook such a study five years ago. In spite of this experience, or perhaps because of it, I am among the most reluctant of composers when it comes to introducing performer-freedom into my composition. Moments of incomplete notation do exist, but only—to quote you—where it is safe."

"Then why have them at all?"

"For the same reason that figured bass was 'filled in' by the performer. As you know, solo parts plus *basso continuo*, reasonably insured the harmonic result. Figured bass was never conceived as a performer-freedom but as a form of shorthand for composer and performer; one avoids cluttering up the score with unessentials. Today our scores are more cluttered. Schoenberg invented H⁻ and N⁻ to clarify the *Notenbild* (a makeshift device, to be sure). This brings me to the notational dilemma of the 1940's and 1950's: the precise notation which results in imprecise performance. Can we speak at all of precise notation if the practical realization can but approximate the complexities on the page? The dilemma lies in the need to notate every minute detail . . . Take a rubato. Here is a comparatively vague notation:

The accelerando, ritardando, written out would produce:

This seemingly precise notation puts the performer in a strait jacket. It is a translation of the supple into the realm of the rigid. A rigid rubato: contradiction in terms. Imagine asking the performer to feel a moment 'out of time,' as it were, when it is notated slavishly 'in time.' Similarly, an effect of, say, chaos, must not be notated in terms of a subtle order. To learn to play the disorderly in orderly fashion is to multiply rehearsal time by one hundred."

"Allow me to be the devil's advocate here. Is not the orderly fashion the only way to play the disorderly? Is not all notation a translation? Is it not a sign of sophistication that this is so? I know of some recent experiments in which the notation simply consists of showing changes in the position of the hands on a keyboard . . ."

"You mean Ligeti's organ pieces."

"Is this not an infinitely more primitive notational concept? It is our traditional notation's ability to translate subtleties like a rubato into measured exactitude which makes it a highly developed tool. Inspired notation is inspired translation, transposition of the inexpressible to the domain of the exact. Take Beethoven's introduction to the last movement in Opus 106, those chords in both hands, that no one can feel as anticipating the beat, because the beat becomes a mere abstraction, as in Webern a hundred years later. I marvel at the surrealism of this notation, implying—without footnotes—the tentative no-beat feeling of a music in search of . . . the fugue theme. Not to mention the ingenious

in the *Grosse Fuge*. As to the complexities of the 1940's and 1950's, agreed, I am yet to hear a precise and spirited performance of Boulez's *Marteau*, instead of all the counting, watching, and approximating. But at least it's all there on paper. The function of notation is not only to serve the immediate performance efficiently, but to keep, to conserve. What will happen to all the aleatory scores in a hundred years?"

"It is perhaps typical and commendable that you, the performer, should be concerned with the composition's immortality. For the composer the issue is how to make it, not how to keep it. New tasks: new performance, new notation. Let me forget the 'masterwork.' We have new problems—some of them perhaps primitive, hence primitively notated. But here I must clear up a misunderstanding. I should like to see traditional notation expanded, not replaced. For instance: I am well aware of the inherent subtlety of the relationship of bar line and beat to the music, which 'overcomes' them. But we also need moments of no bar line and no beat—notes held not by mutual agreement as to the number of counts, but via a spontaneous reaction of one performer to the other. Here is a germ of a performance task capable of much development, and, as yet, far from resolved in the notation-coordination domain: a music where the instruments or voices either individually or in groups, act and react to and against one another, like characters in a play, at times turning the concert stage into a battle-field. This idea proved to be fertile ground for ensemble improvisation. It is easier to improvise in that manner than to compose. On the other hand, one can go much further with it in actual composition. One can develop it into a veritable polyphony of musics, with each music independent of the tempo and pulse of the other. I repeat, this presents a coordination-notation problem. Ives wrestled with this problem, not without reward, but, lacking practical performance experience, he could only derive certain limited effects. Carter found a useful device in 'metrical modulation,' but one that demands concentration by each performer on his own part to the point of shutting out the conflicting pulse of the others; hence, a genuine reacting, in my sense of the word, cannot take place (isn't supposed to, perhaps). Stockhausen's *Gruppen* is the most daring attempt, with its three orchestras, but here the composer relies on the makeshift method of metronome watching, a method which completely isolates one group from the other. I am convinced that genuine coordination must ultimately be obtained via 'reaction,' in other words, via *musical* points of reference, via listening and playing accordingly. Such interplay would constitute a task capable of engaging the performer's entire musical being."

"Is it not perhaps too schizoid a task, forcing upon the performer a role of simultaneous support and opposition? While you ask two players to play *at* each other, you still expect them to play *with* each other."

"Why not? Performance always required the ability to combine, say, passive and active, leading and following. Every downbeat is also an upbeat; our senses take in, enjoy what is just moving into the past, as our mind is shaping the next sounds. Performance also requires the ability to 'interpret' while at the same time allowing the music to 'speak for itself.'[2] And the degree of tension in a performance is dependent on the presence of such a dual effort on the performer's part. A crescendo to a climax is dramatic only if the performer is both the racehorse and the horseman holding the reins. Playing *at* as well as *with* is simply an extension of the duality principle inherent in the drama of musical performance."

"Are there any examples in your recent music which bear out this principle?"

"There is the clarinet, barking in the foreground at a distant tune in the background of *Echoi III*, a piece in which the foreground is much of the time in conflict with the background. But do not stress

---

[2] At the root of this paradox is a phenomenon experienced by all performers: the emergence of the interpreter's originality through identification with the author and submersion in his work.

the 'conflict' aspect of these notions. We are dealing here with a variation of the old idea of different things going on at the same time, and
the somewhat newer idea of what may be called a montage. The unforeseen relationships forming between the mounted elements interest
us today, open up new possibilities. There is a moment in Bach's
Matthew Passion which always struck me as unique and prophetic.
A concert-duet, a setting of a poem of meditative nature, is suddenly
blotted out (without preparation) by the chorus shouting: 'Bind him
not!' Meanwhile, the concert-duet continues under the shouting, un-
perturbed; a form of superimposition, this; a montage of two musics,
that stand in opposition to one another, yet miraculously relate, the
way everything relates if one but finds the key, the nonsense can make
sense and 'open doors' in the hands of genius."

"You mentioned the notation-coordination difficulties arising with
the realization of these ideas. Can you show this on paper?"

"It would take the space of a book to do it."

"You mentioned the need for notation to expand, as indeed it does
today. Is this in the direction of the performer's choice, in the direction
of 'less notation'?"

"A hundred different composers will devise a hundred different
ways. But the new approach to notation can certainly not be equated
with 'avoidance of notation.' Moreover, granting the performer limited
areas of freedom and choice is primarily a formal and textural, not
a notational idea."

"When one looks at the beautiful calligraphy, the graphic originality
of recent scores, is it not as if the notation, the 'writing' of the score
had become an end unto itself?"

"An end perhaps not, but here too, we have a *performance* of
sorts . . ."

"What did you mean earlier by 'moments of incomplete notation'?"

"Unessentials to be filled in by the performer."

"I meant to ask then what could possibly be unessential in a composition, outside of the filling in of a self-evident harmony (as in
figured bass)."

"Take a very fast run, for example, low to high and back to low:
lowest and highest notes may be essential. Intermediate notes may,
under certain circumstances (tempo, style) be unessential:

Leave it as above, and there is immediate clarity regarding the important low and high notes. The performer will realize that the in-between notes need hardly be discernible; the seemingly sketchy notation actually clarifies. I mentioned the barking of the clarinet in *Echoi*. This is to be done by way of a tone distortion, rendering pitches unrecognizable. Hence, I do not write them in, I indicate the approximate height, but erase the staff lines:

In his *Tempi Concertati*, Berio uses the word 'tutta' to indicate that the percussionist is to hit everything, as fast as possible; try to notate this exactly, and you force the percussionist to wrestle with an unessential: the 'order' in which these instruments are to be hit; the resulting performance will seem studied, whereas the effect in the composer's mind was one of abandonment, of eruption. Of course, choices allotted to the performer need not be confined to such detail."

"Where draw the line? At what point does the performer begin to be smothered by unsolicited freedoms, handed to him with a gesture of: '*You* do it.' "

"Never draw the line and say: 'beyond this line there is no art.' But I sympathize with you. Many a new task is an old, or worse, a poor task in disguise. It sounds good in theory, fails in practice. Desk-experiment one may call it; choices allotted to the performer by a composer who has no live experience with performance problems, and who works out a new task like a chess problem. Freedom—choice—dangerous words. Yet the aleatory idea is no idle invention, and quite naturally follows the serial idea. In fact the two complement one another, share the basic premise of an ingenious 'pre-ordering,' which guarantees a particular result. Both involve a *canvassing* of possibilities, which is always in danger of deteriorating into a cataloguing of possibilities, or games of numerology. Both run the risk of self-deceit, serial music in the direction of a would-be order, aleatory music in the direction of a would-be freedom. In our most recent music the two techniques join forces, producing perhaps the most interesting 'laboratory situation' of all times."

"And the music sounds like a 'laboratory situation' some of the time."

"I would not 'object to all this, on principle.' Object if you will, but not on principle. Object if you must to the extra work without extra credit demanded of the performer by the most extreme aleatoric music. Here a situation of 'musical indeterminacy' may well oblige you to decide for yourself what, where, and when to play, perhaps even write out your own part. In the program book there will be no mention of this 'overlapping' of performance and composition. One might call it 'Action-music,' or even, if you wish, 'Gebrauchsmusik.' "[3]

"How closely related are your improvisations to the situation of musical indeterminacy?"

"The latter lays the emphasis on the 'situation' giving birth to the performance. Chamber improvisation lays the emphasis on the 'performance' resulting from the situation, and puts the responsibility for the choices squarely on the shoulders of the performer. It by-passes the composer. It is composition become performance, *performer's music*."

"Age of performance, laboratory obsessed!"

"Yes! 'All the world's a performance.' A monkey performs, lovers perform, Picasso's drawings are a marvel of performance, and the President of the United States performs his office. The word is growing old under my pen. Give me young words . . ."

"Like: situation, event, statement, variant, resultant, parameter?"

"These are 'borrowed' words. One uses them and blushes a little."

"I wonder why you neglected to mention 'chance' in this essay?"

"Quite by chance, I assure you . . ."

---

[3] In a number of Cage's compositions one may play as much or as little of the music as is convenient, use all instruments or only a few, depending on available performance time and personnel.

1963

THE PERFORMER'S POINT OF VIEW

LEONARD STEIN

A STRIKING phenomenon in our time is the wealth of emerging experimental techniques which, in the arts particularly, have tended to foster widespread misunderstanding of the contemporary idiom. This confusion becomes even more apparent when one deals with the communication, always tenuous at best, between composer and performer. New methods of notation have had to be devised by composers in order to define new modes of thought and traditional notation has in some cases had to be amplified by other, often very unusual, symbols, which themselves require further verbal explanation. The search for definitive notations has become a major preoccupation of nearly every significant contemporary composer, since it now may happen that each of his works will possess its own morphology.

Little wonder, then, that when first faced with a new score of great apparent ambiguity the performer's reactions to the music may be seriously inhibited, and he may be discouraged from playing it at all. Although he no longer thinks of "interpreting" a work in the willful manner of an older style, he must still convey with some facility of technique and a degree of personal conviction an identification with the work at hand, based, first of all, on a faithful adherence to the directives, as he understands them, of the composer.

I believe that it was Busoni who, in his *Entwurf einer neuen Ästhetik der Tonkunst* (1907), pointed out that the act of notating music is actually one of transcription: that the performer's interpretation of this notation is yet one step further removed from the source of original inspiration, and that this compounds the difficulty of transliterating a system of symbols transcribed from the mind of the composer to that of the performer who, in turn, has to transmute what he sees into action and then into sound. In addition, it is only as a result of measuring the meanings of these symbols in any given period against their previous meanings that the performer arrives at a comprehensible and convincing performance. The conveyance of the composer's intentions by means of his notational system, according to what we know of his music in general—his choice of vocabulary, structural syntax, instrumental treatment, expressive nuances, etc.—produces what we call his sense of *style*. In past epochs this style was usually transmitted directly by the composer as performer, or by his disciples. It was the product of an oral rather than a written tradition, with the accompanying danger of increasing distortion or "updating" to please modern tastes.

In periods of more or less "common practice," clearly understood notational symbols represented certain definite relationships among pitches, durations, dynamics, and modes of attack, defined by regularly ordered harmonic progressions interacting with metrical accents, rhythmic phrasing, and tempo, to produce larger structures. The individual composer was called upon merely to designate certain deviations from common practice or to suggest subtleties of execution, if he so desired. In twentieth century composition, however, where each situation may be unique, where details proliferate in every direction, where primary lines cannot always be distinguished from those of secondary interest, where, as one says, microcosmic details may subvert macrostructure (see George Rochberg's "Indeterminacy in the New Music" in *The Score*, January, 1960), no such norm of common notational practice seems to exist that might lead to an immediate recognition of the composer's intentions. (Naturally this is not unwelcome to certain contemporaries who delight in such ambiguities, or who desire that their notation function in a purely "objective" manner once launched.) It would thus appear that nowadays each musical occurrence demands its own special description, and that only through considerable experience and exposure to new methods can the performer achieve some insight into contemporary practices or styles.

Fortunately, the performer of our day has considerable opportunity to become acquainted with modern practices, through the wide distribution of contemporary scores, particularly in Europe where subsidization on a large scale exists; through the availability of a great deal of new music on recordings (especially important in the United States where only a small number of such works are heard in the concert hall), or through the increasing descriptions of their ideas by the composers themselves, in print and lecture. In addition, at the summer seminars in modern composition at Darmstadt, Dartington, Princeton, Tanglewood, etc., students are exposed to new techniques and hear expert performances. In such ways, characteristic traits of new music come to be recognized and so to be absorbed into performance tradition. Fidelity to a contemporary style is further abetted by the close rapport that now often exists between composer and performer, and although not all present-day composers are also performers, a great number can demonstrate with considerable precision their intentions regarding the realization of their music.

To return to the notational problem: the tendency towards greater explicitness increased tremendously under the impact of Schoenberg's careful and detailed markings in both atonal and twelve-tone works,[1] and under Webern's close scrutiny of the smallest musical particle, which directly influenced the post-Webern serialists of the late 1940's to pinpoint all the so-called "parameters" with the greatest possible accuracy. Within the extremes of totally organized music a preoccupation with detail seemed, on first appearance at any rate, to allow little opportunity for flexibility of interpretation and to offer, on the contrary, only insuperable roadblocks to a satisfactory realization. That totally determined music was prevented from breaking down into complete indeterminacy by sheer weight of complexity (as feared by certain writers, such as Adorno and Rochberg), was due to the inability of the human mechanism (i.e. the performer) to react "totally" in either a physical or psychological way to the demands of such music.

Other composers, recognizing the impossibility of restricting so completely the responses of the performer, provided him with a "safety valve" by mixing into their works elements conducive to a more approximate and spontaneous way of playing, notated with symbols of a "qualitative" rather than a "quantitative" intent. Pioneered by John Cage and his followers, this approach produces such concepts as chance or random performing and, later on, "controlled choice." At its extreme stage, the performer was advised merely to fill in the details of a generalized line within a certain length of time, or to complete a musical structure and its succession of events.

If any one type of notation may be said to predominate at the present moment, it is that of "total control" mixed with "freedom of choice"—the age-old dichotomy of determinism versus freedom of will. For the performer, the attempt to find a path amid this notational Scylla and Charybdis has brought new problems into existence, whose solution might conceivably lead to a schizoid state in which the interaction of compulsive exactitude and permissive freedom could result in simultaneous attitudes of carelessness towards the controlled elements and a confined and repetitive response to spontaneity in playing.

Widely varying approaches to this "dialectic" of notation may be observed in the evolution of many prominent contemporary composers.

[1] In his *Five Pieces for Orchestra*, Op. 16 (1909), Schoenberg first used brackets to denote principal parts. In the *Four Orchestral Songs*, Op. 22, signs were devised, the *Hauptstimme* and *Nebenstimme*, to be used in every ensemble work thereafter. Beginning with the *Five Piano Pieces*, Op. 23, Schoenberg prefaced nearly every composition with an explanation of his special symbols, pertaining not only to touch and accent but also to the shifting within the bar of downbeat and upbeat.

For example, in the works of Stockhausen—particularly in his piano pieces[2]—steady and successive changes of notation have occurred as the result of his search for the correct morphological form of each composition. Thus, *Piano Piece I* (1953) is extremely detailed and rigidly serialized; *Piece V* (1954)—the first of a second set, not yet published—possesses a far greater flexibility of notation to indicate fluctuating tempos, unmeasured note values, and long pauses; while *Piece XI* (published in 1957) combines both free and rigid methods of notation, contrasting imprecise "time fields" with strictly managed rhythmic proportions.

In Boulez likewise we find changes of notational processes taking place from one composition to the next.[3] One may compare the generally serialized "closed" structure of his Second Sonata for Piano (1948)—influenced particularly by some of the rhythmic organizations of Olivier Messiaen—with the "open" and very flexible construction of his Third Sonata (begun in 1957, though not yet published in its entirety); or the "collective improvisation" of parts of *Pli selon pli*—the two sections published as *Improvisation sur Mallarmé* in 1958—with the completely structured serialization of *Structures I* for two pianos (dating from 1952). It would appear that both Stockhausen and Boulez proceeded from an earlier phase of post-Webern serialization, by way of Messiaen's influence—particularly the latter's *Mode de valeur et d'intensités*—through various phases of increasing flexibility in the handling of details and over-all structure.

Structures I represents one of the best-known realizations of the earlier, first phase of contemporary notation, that of relating the various musical components by a "strictly serialized" process. Various durational, intensity, and attack sets are "derived" from the original pitch set and its permutations. As György Ligeti notes,[4] certain difficulties arise for the performers, which may be characteristic of much serialized music. Although the pitch set offers no problem, since the pitches themselves are completely unambiguous, the durations, ordered

[2] Ten of eleven planned piano pieces have been completed by Stockhausen since 1953—the latest, No. x, in 1961—although only I-IV and XI have been published. There would seem to be some reason to believe that notational problems, as also in the case of the Third Sonata by Boulez, have been at least partly responsible for delaying the completion of the project.

[3] Actually it is a difficult matter to trace direct influences between Stockhausen and Boulez, since each composer seems to have pursued his own development in a different manner. According to Stockhausen's own description—in his article in *Die Reihe* and in my discussions with him—one senses a purposive process of gradual evolution (similar to the one expressed by Henri Pousseur); whereas with Boulez there seems to be a kind of alternation of rigid near-experimental processes carried to their extreme (as in *Polyphonie X* and *Structures*) with those of utmost flexibility, which often incorporate some of the "gains" of the former.

[4] *Die Reihe*, IV.

in purely arithmetical arrangements (from one to twelve 32nd-notes) despite the fact that they are precisely measurable, change with the tempos and become increasingly difficult to measure in quicker movement. In addition, the intensities and attacks, derived in even more factitious ways, assume a great deal of ambiguity because they can only function approximately and in relation to other "parameters." Thus the various sets cannot be treated on a basis of equivalence. The role of the performer becomes that of one second removed; once he has mastered his responses as accurately as possible, according to the details of serialization, he must then strive to articulate the sections and discover what contrasts exist. A knowledge of the different uses of the parametrical sets in the various sections of the work and how they are distributed between the two pianos may help to achieve articulation and balance. The larger structure of which he is aware, as well as changes in tempo, density, emphasis on certain tones—even the appearance of occasional motives and imitations—may be considered by the performer to be more than just fortuitous happenings, and should also be taken into account so that he does not react as a mere automaton but discovers, instead, relationships of a higher order than those inherent in the "serial" system itself. As Ligeti concludes, the performers of this work should control the elements as far as possible, be aware of the articulations between the larger structures, and realize that it is possible to achieve some variances among separate performances.

Stockhausen's first *Piano Piece* would also seem to qualify as a "totally serialized" work. Although definite meters are given for each bar, its "irrational" subdivisions (11:10, 7:5, etc.) often seem completely contradictory and defy any attempt on the part of the performer to measure the time. The tempo here, as in all the four pieces of this set, is determined by the "smallest note value" to be played "as fast as possible." Thus there is no actual tempo "parameter." Nevertheless the rhythmic proportions may be decided by choosing a fixed metronomic mark for a constant unit, which could be the quarter or eighth of a regular "rational" measure (such as m. 3 in Ex. 1). Supposing the "regular" eighth to be equal to MM. 120, then the first measure changes tempo from 132 to 185 (see parentheses in Ex. 1).

In the course of this piece the eighth would then fluctuate between MM. 90 and 185, although, for practical purposes, one could count in larger or smaller units at certain places. Such tempo "fluctuations," of course, bring up new problems, but they are certainly of a type to be found in many other contemporary works, such as *Calligraphie* by

Ex. 1. Stockhausen, *Klavierstücke*

Keijiro Satō (see Ex. 2) and *Anaklasis* by Krzysztof Penderecki, both of which use fluctuating "tempo lines."

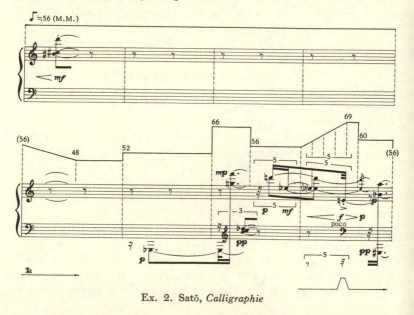

Ex. 2. Satō, *Calligraphie*

Other prominent composers, such as Ernst Krenek, Luigi Nono, and Milton Babbitt, have also devised their own notational methods of presenting serialized relationships. In his *Sechs Vermessene* for piano (1958), Krenek notates irrational time relationships by wavy stems within measures of equal value (see Ex. 3). His *Sestina* and *Quaestio temporis* utilize some of the most complicated serialized interrelationships among parameters yet devised—discussed at length in his article, "Extents and Limits of Serial Techniques" in the Princeton Seminar issue of the *Musical Quarterly* (April 1960).

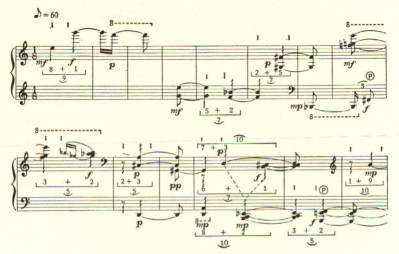

Ex. 3. Krenek, *Sechs Vermessene*

As one of the main results of the problematic responses to the rigid quantization of "serial" music, a second phase of modern notation has come about. In his article in *Die Reihe* III, Stockhausen shows how increasing notational complexity may lead to a state where the performer tends to commit an increasing number of errors. The imprecise "time fields" (as he calls them) resulting from these errors may be organized on another level by using approximate "qualitative" notation rather than one denoting exact quantities. The type of notation he uses for these time fields is derived from grace notes of former practice, and consists of small undifferentiated note values. Appearing for the first time in his second cycle of *Piano Pieces*, these small notes are to be played (according to the hand-written instructions of the composer) "as fast as possible, but at all times as clear and important as the other notes. The higher these notes, the faster they are to be played; if the interval is greater, their duration becomes a bit longer, and vice versa. Groups of little notes are *outside* of the measured time: ad lib. (they are put *between* the measured values)." The most important aim of these pieces, he concludes, is to "break the time continuum of metronomic measures by different events which are unmeasured (if we think by the watch)—or better, measured by *action* ('as fast as possible,' different kinds of attacks, and so forth)."

In *Zeitmasse* Stockhausen goes even further in "breaking the time-continuuum" by indicating various degrees of time fields—"as fast as possible," "as slow as possible" (depending on the breath control of the player), "fast-slowing down" and "slow-quickening"—indications which, at times, even occur simultaneously, so that still greater imprecision results.

Similar qualitative and approximative notational devices appear also in the two published *Improvisation* sections of Boulez' *Pli selon pli*. For instance, we find special indications for fluctuating tempos—used at first in the fifth movement of *Le Marteau sans Maître* where the extremes of acceleration and retard from a basic tempo are indicated thus: $\quart = 66 \swarrow 80 \nearrow 120$ for *fermate* of various lengths, for numbered degrees of acceleration (0 to 4) within a variable tempo, for free recitative-like passages marked "Senza tempo." There are also other signs that aid in delineating the "collective improvisatory" style of this work.

A further development of this second phase of notation is discussed quite thoroughly by Pousseur in his "Zur Methodik" ("Outline of a Method") in *Die Reihe* III. In his music he "seeks a qualitative notation of time-phenomena as we perceive them. Such a notation, relieved of the demand for absolute quantitative exactness," he asserts, "would make use of every possible and acceptable threshold of approximation." He doubts that a performer, "in order to attain a really satisfying interpretation," must reduce what are truly qualitative aspects of music to exclusively numerical communication. His search for the "semantic kernel" of this new style leads him to the adoption of a notation which attempts to define "qualitative aperiodicity" by a systematic use of grace notes. But it is this very systematic attempt, producing no less than eighteen distinct note symbols in his *Exercices pour Piano* (published in 1959 and consisting of *Impromptu* and *Variations II*), which leads to the paradoxical necessity to set precise limitations to the performer's freedom in deciding the different qualitative values.

In his latest piano piece, *Caractères* (first performed in 1961), Pousseur introduces other symbols, including inexact metric indications, to represent values which, as he states in the introduction, are to be "felt as units, whose relations are of a qualitative nature." The ultimate difficulty of recognizing the composer's style through his choice of notation, mentioned earlier as one of the performer's basic problems, is acknowledged by Pousseur in his article when he concedes that "this notation presupposes in the interpreter both an understanding of the *semantic kernel* from which all structural principles are derived (i.e. integral aperiodicity) and a clear idea of what, as a means of fulfilling this demand, is in fact possible with our sensory apparatus."

The method of performing *Caractères*—as the instructions say: "One can begin with any one of the six double pages . . ."—leads us to a third phase of performance problems which, although not necessarily dealing with new notational devices other than those already discussed, presents the performer with the necessity of choosing the elements and their succession, offered to him within greater or lesser limits by the composer, in order to collaborate on the determination of the overall structure of a piece.

The best-known work of this type is *Piano Piece XI* by Stockhausen (published in 1957), a "random" piece of unusual graphic appearance, consisting of nineteen scattered fragments in a "directionless time field" (as the composer describes it) which can be played in any order that the performer chooses. However, certain indications after each one of the fragments delimit the way in which the succeeding fragment may be played: according to tempo (marked 1 to 6, fast to slow), dynamics (a range of six, between ppp and ff), and attacks (also six). Although these three "formants" are of approximate values, depending to a great extent on the capabilities of the performer, the latter—who after sufficient practice will probably not play "at random" anyway, as the composer urges him to do—may feel considerably restricted in achieving sufficient contrasts in the piece by the limitations imposed upon him by the composer's instructions.

Demanding similar "collaboration" on the part of the performer, but of vastly greater complexity, is the Third Sonata for piano by Boulez (begun in 1957). The components of its five *formants* (or movements) can be arranged in various ways by the performer, but are determined to a great extent by a method of "directed choice"—rather than one of randomness—controlled by the composer. The apogee of this method is reached in the third *formant*—called *Constellation*—in which the choice of certain "paths" determines alternatives of tempo and succession. Its numerous segments, designated as "blocs" or "points," occur with such rapid fluctuation that the performer is under constant strain to preserve any sense of direction or form. Some of the segments occupy but a few seconds, yet change tempo on nearly every note.

This work represents as well as any I know the present relationship between performer and composer. Boulez, in his article on the Third Sonata (published elsewhere in the present issue of this journal) admits that he confronts the performer with a condition of unpredetermined choice containing so many ramifications that no total determination is possible. Citing a description from Kafka of man's isolated position, he implies that the performer is placed in a labyrinth within which he must construct his own architecture.

In a discerning observation on this work, Ligeti notes that "the new freedom of the performer is not one of improvising . . . but a sufferance only, in which he selects out of the list of structural possibilities drawn up beforehand by the composer the appropriate ones." He contends that this is, in effect, only a superficial aspect of freedom.

A study of this sort would hardly be complete without some mention of a "fourth phase" of contemporary performance problems, that of more or less complete unpredictability based, to a great extent, on visual or graphic notation. This phase has been thoroughly exploited in the United States for more than a decade by John Cage and his followers; more recently it has caught on in Europe, as well, in works by such composers as Roman Haubenstock-Ramati and Sylvano Bussotti. Its principles, moreover, have been incorporated into works of quite different tendency, often alongside of more traditional notational devices such as the *Hodograph* by Earle Brown, which uses, in the composer's description, both "explicit" and "implicit" notations.

The performer of contemporary music, as can be seen from this very limited glance at various "phases" of modern notation, is faced with an overwhelming richness of challenges and apparent contradictions from all sides. But, at the same time, few periods in recent music history have granted him so great an opportunity to participate in the creation of new musical idioms.

1963

NOTES ON THE PERFORMANCE OF CONTEMPORARY MUSIC

CHARLES WUORINEN

DISCUSSIONS OF contemporary music which reach a sufficiently "practical" point to be concerned with performance usually emphasize the "extreme difficulty" of modern music and tend to regard its performers as "virtuosi" of the highest order, in whom an altruistic sense has been, additionally, developed to an abnormal degree. Implicit is the notion that the presumed difficulty is "inevitable," that it cannot be removed because of the directions that composers' concerns have taken over the past half-century, that these directions point toward a not far distant moment of strangulation where the tape recorder will replace the live player, and that meanwhile we had all better be grateful to those players who actually do suffer through the process of learning new music.

All this can be evaporated with the realization that new music is in fact not so difficult to perform as people think, and that the problems experienced by performers in dealing with it are the result of their having been trained in a tradition of no relevance to its performance requirements. Moreover, I have been emboldened by personal experience to conclude that even the most difficult new music is far from approaching the limits of human performance capacities: given sufficiently efficient instruments, anything that can be heard (in the sense of "musically perceived") can, I am convinced, be played. Beyond raising interesting side issues (for example, the conclusion that the virtues of the electronic medium must necessarily lie in other domains than that of mere capacity to "do" what human beings "cannot do"), this indicates that the present demands of most contemporary music are no more "impractical" than those of any virtuoso music of the past—less, in fact, than some. Indeed, it could hardly be otherwise, for composers can only conceive performance demands in terms of (at most) slight extensions of the going performance practice. "Unplayable" really means "unhearable," and can therefore be applied as accurately to the electronic medium as to the instrumental. And it may be said that this definition renders most old music "unplayable"—if the lack of comprehension demonstrated in this area by most players is taken into account.

With respect to the supposed rhythmic difficulties of contemporary music (the area most often cited as the seat of unsolvable performance problems), two examples from the past seem relevant. Both have certain similarities to modern music; having participated in performances of both of them, I can attest that their demands are no less formidable than any made today. The first, part of *Le Greygnour Bien* of Matheus de Perusio (c. 1400), is hard enough to realize accurately when written in "modern" score form with all values referable to a bar line.

Ex. 1

But when one considers the analog in modern notation of this example as written in the 14th century,

Ex. 2

and further considers that there was no score, it becomes clear that the capacities of the Avignon musicians who performed it were in no way inferior to our own. (Incidentally, the musicological conceit—that this music, because of its "complexity," is "decadent"—is based on the premise that the symmetries of music of the recent past constitute a norm against which everything else, old or new, is to be measured. This premise, among other things, assumes that periodicity, exact durational and articulative symmetry, and binary division of duration are "basic" —an assumption not only contrary to fact and logically unacceptable but also belied by its difficulty of realization in practice: if these divisions were basic, why would beginning students, and many professionals, find such particular difficulty in playing "even" note values?)

A second example, from Morley's *Plaine and Easie Introduction to Practicall Musicke* (1597), is not even a piece of art music: as a teaching piece whose performance was supposed to enable students to cope with the going rhythmic demands, it demonstrates impressively that our conception of rhythmic difficulty must be based on our teaching. Presented first in modern form,

Ex. 3

and then in a modern analog of old notation (but still in a score form not provided in the original) (Ex. 4),

Ex. 4

this excerpt shows that its performance is difficult only if one plays the sevens or the fives *against* "basic" binary divisions of the beat; if, instead, one knows from one's training how to divide a given quantity of time into any number of parts, as the old musicians did, i.e. how fast septuplets, etc., are in a given *unity,* there is no special problem of execution.

These examples clearly illustrate that the measurement of musical time is difficult only when incorrect or irrelevant definitions are applied to musical situations: rhythmic difficulties are "psychological." It seems helpful, therefore, to offer a suggestion about the most profitable way for a performer to train himself to handle contemporary rhythmic situations. The proper execution of the so-called "irrational" divisions (quintuplets, septuplets, etc.) is problematic only because most players are unaware of the relation between their speeds and that of a "basic" binary-divided beat "against" which they are placed. Memorization of these relations is easily accomplished by practice, in which the largest common subdivision between the "irrational" and the "basic" beat is counted (e.g., quarter-note quintuplets practiced by counting quintuple subdivisions of the unaltered quarter note, with articulations every four counts). Such practice leads to the memorization of relations between given speeds, such that ultimately it becomes irrelevant to speak, say, of "septuplets" in a given "tempo"; one really thinks of speeds related as 7:4, and plays accordingly. Such memorization is no more difficult than that which permits us to discover a speed related to a "basic tempo" as 2:1, e.g., to play 8th notes in 4/4. Indeed, the rigidity of binary-related speed-proportions renders their initial mastery far more difficult than is that of speeds related as 3:2, 5:4, 5:6, 7:4, 7:6, etc., where the proportions, while still superparticular, are nevertheless sufficiently complex to allow much greater real inaccuracy in their execution to be tolerable to a human auditor.

Only after "irrational" divisions have been memorized by a performer, thus enabling him to produce them without fuss, will he be in a position to ask a profounder question about contemporary rhythmic practice: what does a composer intend by a given "irrational" division? There are at least two possible interpretations of all such situations, and our notation unfortunately fails utterly to distinguish between them. The two are: (1) that the irrational group—this is especially likely when one such group occurs with a different other—is being used to assure an asymmetrical sequence of attacks; and (2) that the group is to represent the (perhaps local) establishment of a new speed, which in turn may be to set up a tension against either (a) the beat, or (b) the measure, phrase, or longer structural unit, or combinations of these. Clearly, much less literal accuracy in execution is required under (1) than under (2), and indeed, a wholly different manner of performance is implied. And since these two "basic" possible interpretations are in no way mutually exclusive, complex interpretative problems arise when the compositorial intent is not clarified with respect to this issue. Composers generally show too little awareness of these differences, but since the semantics of the notation they use is itself incapable of such niceties, they are hardly to be blamed for failing to express differentiations that exist outside the resources of this linguistic system. Nevertheless, a greater awareness on their part of such differences would eventually result in the development of a more precisely differentiated system of rhythmic representation.

Assuming players who have overcome individual rhythmic and articulative difficulties, we arrive at what is really a more crucial aspect of contemporary performance: the accurate realization of ensemble rhythm. Here the problem of accurate and meaningful realization (which are not always identical) seems very little related to degrees of "complexity" as they appear on paper.[1] Consider, for instance, this straightforward excerpt from Milton Babbitt's *Composition for Four Instruments* (Ex. 5),

[1] If it were necessary, this alone would demonstrate the complete imbecility of the premises on which, for example, Stockhausen's *Klavierstuck XI* is based.

Ex. 5

which nevertheless is quite as demanding as the following from Stefan Wolpe's Quartet for oboe, cello, percussion, and piano, whose notated "complexities" appear much greater.

Ex. 6

In both cases, meaningful representation is only possible if each player knows the total score, and therefore can "hear the piece." Given that, both are equally simple of realization. But only in performances rehearsed far beyond the minimal levels established by those "professional musicians" for whom the mere public approximation of works is sufficient can such issues be met.

In the realization of contemporary ensemble rhythms, a new "chamber music style" must develop, and indeed already has.[2] Such a style is based on the transfer of that rubato which used to be the province of the individual player—and which is as necessary (though in new domains) in the performance of contemporary music as in any other—to the entire playing group: a "collective" rubato, unthinkable to musicians who view the art in terms of individual aggrandisement.

Speed of articulation in contemporary music presents major problems to some performers. Yet it cannot be said that any known music of today contains speeds in excess of those reached in the virtuoso writing of the past century; indeed, extreme speeds are by no means the exclusive province of the recent past. Returning to Morley, we find a passage,

Ex. 7

in which the tactus, transcribed here as a half note, may be assumed to proceed at about mm 48. At such a speed the 8th notes, here subdivided in 4, are at mm 192, a rate fast enough in itself, but even more extraordinary when one considers the (by modern standards) slow-speaking instruments that probably performed the piece. If, moreover, one takes literally Morley's instruction that the lower parts be *sung* to solmization syllables, the virtuosity required becomes altogether staggering. We must therefore put down this difficulty, as we do complaints about the difficulty of "disjunct" motion, to the intransigence of habits acquired by most players in their training. It is this, rather, that we must criticize.

Considering the irrelevance of the musical materials by which players are taught to "master" their instruments today, it is really a marvel that performances of contemporary music are possible at all. Quite apart from the fact that to teach playing by the use of binary-tonal music unjustifiably elevates that music to the status of a norm, and

---

[2] The performances of the Group for Contemporary Music at Columbia University are based on this premise, and have already begun to show—albeit sporadically—the fruits of such an approach.

thereby makes it difficult to comprehend music composed in other systems, current training inadequately prepares performers to cope with the most common problems of performance today. In general, the musical language of the present moment avoids binary symmetry and interrelates its pitches in more specific and detailed ways than does the music in which most players are trained. It would certainly be profitable then, to acquaint players from the start of their education with other common kinds of pitch and temporal articulation. When one suggests this, however, it is objected that other situations are less "basic" than the binary-conjunct, and that their investigation must be therefore deferred to a more "advanced" stage. This is absurd, as any consideration of the past beyond the most recent 200 years will demonstrate. For instance, the introduction of duple rhythm into the art music of medieval Europe met with great resistance, apparently because the musical minds of that time had been so trained in a rhythmic system built of longs and shorts (hence, an entirely ternary system) that the idea of a succession of short even pulses was quite inconceivable. Magister Lambert (*c.* 1240) remarks:

> From this it appears that an imperfect longa can be executed only in connection with a following or preceding brevis, since a longa and a brevis . . . together always complete a perfection. Therefore, if someone were to ask whether a mode or a natural song can be formed by imperfect longae exclusively just in the same way as it can be formed by perfect longae, the approved answer is: no, since nobody can sing a succession of pure imperfect longae.[3]

Or, in other words, a succession of articulations in binary proportion —such as is now called "basic" by music teachers—was simply "unplayable" in the conceptual-practical terms of the 13th-century musician.

I hope to be forgiven for the banality of remarking that no significant, or even accurate, performance is possible without the performers' perception of the structure which their performance realizes. Needless to say, the "analysis" that makes good performance possible may have no more relation to compositional intent than a comparably successful theoretic analysis,[4] but in the one case as in the other, it is optimally

---

[3] Willi Apel, *Notation of Polyphonic Music,* pub. by The Medieval Academy of America.

[4] A proper use of the word "analysis" would restrict its application to explications of significantly "heard" structure. Unfortunately, however, there are many purely descriptive treatments of pieces (or of their notation) that call themselves analyses—and it is to these that I refer. The relation of all this to performance is further clouded by the fact that there are other discussions of particular pieces which, while they may not demonstrate the contextual functioning of relations within a work, nevertheless elucidate general procedures of which particular works being discussed are instances; it is this kind of theoretical generalizing—also often miscalled analysis—that seems to me "valuable outside of rehearsal," since it acquaints the performer with the general procedural framework within which the piece he is playing functions.

desirable to digest those intentions of the composer, and those opinions he has about the nature of his piece, that are not already indicated in his score—and hence can only be received from him in person. Since most of our musical life is spent in trying to unravel ambiguities resulting from the fact that no score or performance ever represents the complete intent of its creator, it is interesting to reflect on what would happen to performance if musical notation could be rendered even as unambiguous as verbal language.

In any event, it is extremely difficult to say just what goes into the kind of "analysis" necessary for informed performance. It is possible to observe, however, that the type of analysis generally presumed to have value in "theoretical" explication is often useless in the preparation of a performance. The theoretic kind of analysis is usually devoted to displaying relationships that are sufficiently unobvious as to require that they be pointed at by other than aural means in order to be perceived. (This should not be taken as any criticism of such relations: it has been observed that any relation once exhibited can be heard, and in any case it is usually not the most apparent relations that are the most significant.) From the performer's point of view, such conventional analyses, while of course generally useful to him outside of rehearsal, nevertheless fail to motivate his manner of playing, since their major part is most often devoted to translating the information presented in a work into another (usually verbal) linguistic medium. The performer, however, needs not translation but direction and focusing. Suppose, for instance, that he is presented with two successive tones to be articulated, registrally separated and unconnected by any slur or similar mark. Given knowledge of the basic premises of the composition, he may know not to associate these two tones into a phrase, since their registral separation may indicate, say, association with different set segments. But suppose the same two tones occur later in the same registral relationship, but this time as a simple adjacency. Here, the performer cannot be blamed for failing to "get" the pun unless the composer indicates (for example by a slur) that this time the tones *are* to be associated; the composer will have failed in notating the piece if such an ambiguity remains. Whether or not the performer, in such a situation, should still be able to make the distinction is not a question I propose to consider, since it can only arise when the composer has not been sufficiently professional in doing *his* job.

It is of utmost importance, for example, to know that the plucked piano notes in Donald Martino's Trio for violin, clarinet, and piano are present not for "coloristic" reasons, but to differentiate elements of structure.[5] It is not of crucial necessity to a successful performance of

[5] But it is equally essential to recognize that Martino did not pick pizzicato piano as a timbre because he *disliked* its sound.

this work, however, to know precisely which set segments are being presented through this particular form of articulation—apparently because given this knowledge, there is very little one can do in the moment of performance to project it—beyond putting on a knowing, rather than an exotic, expression.

A different situation exists with Peter Westergaard's Variations for Six Players, written for, and recently performed by, the Group for Contemporary Music. Here the remarks made above about Martino's piano-plucking apply not only to the timbrally differentiated articulations in the piano, but to "special" sounds required of all the other instruments (Ex. 8).

Ex. 8

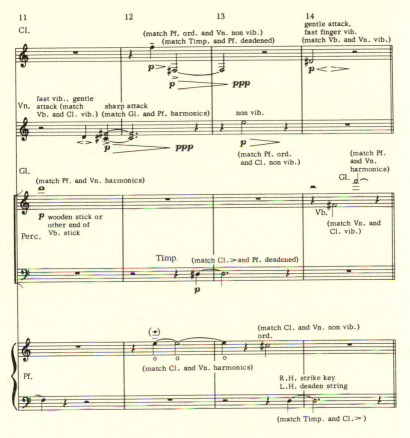

Ex. 8 (cont.)

It is necessary to know that the timbral differentiations in this excerpt all have structural function. But here a more detailed knowledge than is needed in the Martino is useful, because is *can* be projected in performance. Each register proceeds in half-aggregates, while the totality of registers does so as well, and the diversity of timbres and articulations required from each instrument serves, within the ambitus covered by each, to mark off the registers. An intelligent performance is not possible unless the players know these matters and can therefore match the several types of articulation they must each produce to similar types in similar registers in other instruments. Moreover, intelligent players will perceive that in this excerpt, their individual parts have the same hexachordal content as the registral collections and the four total collections: they will therefore attempt internal linear continuity in their individual parts as well. In other words, at least this much "analytic" information is needed about the excerpt before a perform-ance can even begin to attempt to project its elegant three-way continuity.

For the implementation and validation of the various suggestions I have made, the only requisite is the willingness of performers to expend the necessary time on preparation of contemporary music. It is regrettable that the structure of the "professional" musical world is such as to make such expenditure of time difficult. Yet, just as a given status quo has never prevented composers from willing change into being, so the existence of a particular set of circumstances in the "professional" world should never be adduced as a "reason" for not devoting adequate time to preparing new music for performance. It is only when, in this most mundane domain, basic circumstances are questioned, as they are in the acts of composition and performance themselves, that we can approach representations of music (both modern and ancient) worthy of the compositional efforts that have called the music into being. And the present activities of various groups and individuals who manifest such a questioning attitude already show how vast and fruitful a field lies before us.

1964

NOTE VALUES

JOHN MAC IVOR PERKINS

THE EXPLORATION of unconventional rhythmic ideas, and its attendant problems of notation and realization, has become a deep concern for many living composers. Stemming perhaps from a new understanding of the experience and perception of time,[1] such ideas usually constitute an emancipation of intricate or "irrational" duration relationships through multiple simultaneous "artificial division," irregular meter, "rhythmic modulation," incommensurable tempo change and/or analog notation. Emphasis is placed on the expansion of resources and on flexibility, often at the expense of traditional cohesive, unifying and organizing forces, and the musical results are thus roughly analogous to the musical results of those earlier developments in the area of pitch relations called by Schoenberg "the emancipation of dissonance." But while we have now reached a temporary harmonic plateau (despite persistent and persuasive voices of dissatisfaction)[2] in the acceptance of twelve-tone equal temperament, whether serially organized or not, it is evident that the emancipation of rhythmic dissonance is far from complete. Few composers would deny that the rhythmic, even more surely than the harmonic, aspect of our musical language is currently in a state of rapid transition.

In this light, the fact that recent scores employ a confusing variety of notation systems is not surprising. The most prominent systems[3] fall into two categories, reflecting a two-pronged assault on the mechanical symmetry, endless bipartite divisions, "tickiness,"[4] metrical rigidity, one-at-a-time tempo limitation and poverty of duration and speed relationships which served Mozart so well, but which seem now so intolerably and irrelevantly restrictive. In analog notation, the horizontal distance between the noteheads (or other event symbols) is strictly proportional to the intended time-difference of attack (or other event, such as dynamic

---

[1] Robert Erickson, "Time-Relations," *Journal of Music Theory*, Winter 1963, pp. 174–92.

[2] For a recent example see Ben Johnston, "Scalar Order as a Compositional Resource," PERSPECTIVES OF NEW MUSIC, Spring 1964, pp. 56–76. The ideas about rhythm in this article and in Erickson, *op. cit.*, are closely relevant to the present discussion.

[3] A convenient survey is included in Kurt Stone, "Problems and Methods of Notation," PERSPECTIVES OF NEW MUSIC, Spring 1963, pp. 9–31.

[4] Erickson, *op. cit.*

change, timbre change, or release). Hence the name "proportionate notation" for these systems, a name which will not be used here because of the
possibility of confusion: conventional notation presents durational *proportions* more explicitly than does analog notation, and to this is due many of
the practical disadvantages of all analog systems.[5] The use of conventional
notation with numerical, verbal, or other symbolic extensions entails
some disadvantages of its own, however, the most obvious of which is the
cluttering of the page with a profusion of signs which are slow to read.
This compares poorly with the beautiful simplicity of the better analog
notations—a visual and conceptual simplicity which may or may not
lead to more efficient performance. The less obvious limitations of conventional notation are more important,[6] and should if possible be ana-
lyzed in some detail by those students and young composers who find
themselves confronted with a choice.

An easily accomplished but not entirely trivial first step in such an
analysis would be an inventory of available conventional note values.
In theory, an infinite number of duration values, corresponding to the
infinite number of rational fractions of the unit duration in a given tempo,
can of course be expressed in conventional notation, when it is supplemented by proportion symbols such as those employed by the Darmstadt
composers. In practice, a relatively small finite number (about fifty per
duration octave—e.g. between a quarter note and an eighth note) is in
fact available, owing to the difficulties of reading a large number of flags
and executing proportional modifications involving large numbers. Of
these, many are exceedingly rare. The limitations of the accompanying
table (pp. 50–51) have been chosen to approximate the practical limitations at normal tempi: additive values in sixty-fourths are included, as are
proportional modifications involving numbers up to and including fifteen.
In addition, a few of the more important values resulting from the following notational procedures have been listed: (1) the addition of artificial
divisions (a triplet eighth tied to a septuplet eighth, resulting in a duration
equal to thirteen twenty-firsts of a quarter note; such values are fairly
common in practice, but are rarely used as beats or "counters" in rhythmic modulations); (2) the simultaneous or otherwise coordinated employ-
ment of compound and simple meters (the double-dotted dotted note used
as a "counter" by Carter in the Second Quartet, mm. 138–39); (3) the use
of artificial divisions of a higher order than fifteen (the most common of
which is probably 17:16); (4) the nesting of artificial divisions beyond

---

[5] Discussed in Stone, *op. cit.*

[6] Since at present no notation will enable a "complex" rhythmic pattern to be read quickly
and easily, even if, as Charles Wuorinen believes, the difficulties of such patterns are largely
cultural in origin rather than inherent; see his "Notes on the Performance of Contemporary
Music," PERSPECTIVES OF NEW MUSIC, Fall–Winter 1964.

five (a triplet half note within a septuplet, resulting in a duration of sixteen twenty-firsts of a quarter note).

At this point, a word about the details of the particular notation convention employed in this list (and elsewhere) is unfortunately very necessary, not only because the practice of composers has been strikingly inconsistent in this regard, but also because the citation of note values outside a musical or metrical context—as for example in note-value equations used in writing rhythmic modulations—imposes special criteria in the evaluation of notation conventions. In particular, it would be most desirable that, in a given tempo, one and only one duration value be represented by each note-value symbol, the symbol being taken to include its proportional or other modifiers. This criterion does not necessarily apply in practical music notation,[7] and of course its converse is not true, for the variety of symbols available for the expression of each duration is essential to the flexibility of conventional notation. On the other hand, the comparative unexplicitness of the Darmstadt proportion notation[8] does minimize the number of such equivalent symbols, which is sometimes advantageous; and while it is undeniable that this unexplicitness may occasionally lead to confusion in practice[9] (and should in these situations be supplemented in the manner of Carter), there is no reason why it should lead in any situation to an actual ambiguity (in the sense that more than one duration may properly be read for a given symbol). For these reasons, the Darmstadt notation is best suited to the present purposes, and is understood in the following way:

$$\text{duration}\left(\begin{array}{c}\ulcorner x:y \urcorner \\ n\end{array}\right) = \frac{y}{x}\,\text{duration}\,(n)$$

where (n) is any conventional (including dotted) note value. For example, the duration of a quarter note within a bracket marked $5:3$ is *always* equal to three fifths of the duration of an unmodified quarter note in the same tempo. For compactness, the number y is frequently omitted from the symbol, in which case it is assumed (here) to be equal to the next power of two smaller than x.[10] Thus:

[7] The notation used by Easley Blackwood in Music for Flute and Harpsichord is efficient and unambiguous without conforming to this rule: the number which appears after the colon in each case refers to the number of *beats* occupied by the bracketed notes. The meaning of a particular symbol thus depends on its metrical context. The same is true of Hindemith's notation of artificial divisions in compound meter (see below, n. 10).

[8] Stone, *op. cit.*

[9] See Elliott Carter, "Letter to the Editor," *Journal of Music Theory,* Winter 1963, pp. 270–73.

[10] This abbreviation rule corresponds exactly with the method described in Hindemith's *Elementary Training For Musicians,* p. 116, for simple duple meters. Carter has always employed, and has recently urged the general adoption of, a different method (described in *Principles of Music Theory* by Longy-Miquelle; see Carter, *op. cit.*) according to which $\ulcorner 7 \urcorner = 7:8$. The rule behind this would seem to be that y is assumed to equal the power of two which is arithmetically

Number	Standard symbol	duration ♩ = 1/1	duration ♪ = 1.000 (d)	duration, logarithmic $\frac{\log(d)}{\log 2}$	duration, logarithmic × 1200 "cents"	M.M. ♩ = 60	Equivalent symbols
00	♩	1/1	2.000	1.000	1200.0	60	
		20/21	1.905	.9296	1115.5-	63	
	17	16/17	1.882	.9125	1095.0		
01	♩⋯	15/16	1.875	.9069	1088.3	64	
02	15:14	14/15	1.867	.9004	1080.6		
03	14:13	13/14	1.857	.8930	1071.7		
04	13:12	12/13	1.846	.8846	1061.4	65	
05	12:11	11/12	1.833	.8745	1049.4		
06	11:10	10/11	1.818	.8625	1035.0	66	
07	5:9	9/10	1.800	.8480	1017.6		
08	9	8/9	1.778	.8301	996.1		
09	♩‥	7/8	1.750	.8074	968.8		
		20/23	1.739	.7984	958.1	69	
10	15:13	13/15	1.733	.7935	952.2		
11	7:6	6/7	1.714	.7776	933.1	70	
12	13:11	11/13	1.692	.7590	910.8		
13	3:5	5/6	1.667	.7370	884.4	72	
14	11:9	9/11	1.636	.7105	852.6		
15		13/16	1.625	.7004	840.5		
16	5	4/5	1.600	.6781	813.7	75	
		15/19	1.579	.6589	790.7	76	
17	7:11	11/14	1.571	.6521	782.5		
18	9:7	7/9	1.556	.6374	764.9		
19	13:10	10/13	1.539	.6215	745.8	78	
	7	16/21	1.524	.6076	729.2		
20		3/4	1.500	.5850	702.0	80	
21	15:11	11/15	1.467	.5525	663.0		
22	11	8/11	1.455	.5405	648.7		
23	9:13	13/18	1.444	.5305	636.6		
24	7:5	5/7	1.429	.5146	617.5	84	

Table 1

Number	Standard symbol	duration		duration, logarithmic		M.M. ♩ = 60	Equivalent symbols
		♪ = 1/1	♪ = 1.000 (d)	$\frac{\log(d)}{\log 2}$	× 1200 "cents"		
25	5:7	7/10	1.400	.4854	582.5		15:14 5 5
26	13:9	9/13	1.385	.4695	563.4		13:12 13
27		11/16	1.375	.4594	551.3		12:11 8:11
28	11:15	15/22	1.364	.4474	537.0	88	11:10 11 11
29	3	2/3	1.333	.4150	498.0	90	9 3
		21/32	1.313	.3923	470.8		
		15/23	1.304	.3833	460.0	92	
30	10:13	13/20	1.300	.3785	454.2		15:13 5 5
31	7:9	9/14	1.286	.3626	435.1		7:6 7 7
32	11:7	7/11	1.273	.3479	417.5		11 11:12
33		5/8	1.250	.3219	386.3	96	6:5 4:5
34	13	8/13	1.231	.2996	359.5		13:12 13:12
35	9:11	11/18	1.222	.2895	347.4		9 12:11 9
36	5:3	3/5	1.200	.2630	315.6	100	5 10:9 5
37	11:13	13/22	1.182	.2410	289.2		11 11
38	6:7	7/12	1.167	.2224	266.9		9:7 3 3
39	13:15	15/26	1.154	.2064	247.7	104	13:10 13:12 13
40	7	4/7	1.143	.1927	231.2		7:6 7
41		9/16	1.125	.1699	203.9		2:3 8:9
42	9:10	5/9	1.111	.1520	182.4	108	6:5 9
43	10:11	11/20	1.100	.1375	165.0		15:11 5 5
44	11:12	6/11	1.091	.1255	150.6		11 11:9 11
45	12:13	13/24	1.083	.1155	138.6		9:13 3
46	13:14	7/13	1.077	.1069	128.3		13 13
47	14:15	15/28	1.071	.0995	119.4	112	7:5 7 7
48	5 3	8/15	1.067	.0932	111.7		15 3 5 15
		17/32	1.063	.0875	105.0		
		15/29	1.034	.0489	58.7	116	
00		1/2	1.000	.0000	0.0	120	

Table 1 (Cont.)

$$\lceil 3 \rceil = 3:2$$
$$\lceil 5 \rceil = 5:4$$
$$\lceil 7 \rceil = 7:4\text{[10]}$$
$$\lceil 9 \rceil = 9:8$$
$$\lceil 11 \rceil = 11:8$$
$$\lceil 13 \rceil = 13:8\text{[10]}$$
$$\lceil 15 \rceil = 15:8\text{[10]}$$
$$\lceil 17 \rceil = 17:16$$

etc.

(Even-numbered values of x are superfluous in out-of-context citations of note values, and dangerously ambiguous even in context if the y value is not also given.)[11]

The accompanying table, then, presents the symmetrical scale-like array of duration values available to the user of conventional notation. The axis of symmetry in this particular duration-octave falls between note values number 24 and 25, and would be represented by an irrational duration equal to $\sqrt{2}$ times the duration of the eighth note. Thus, for example, $\flat$ and $\overline{\flat}^3$ are symmetrically placed around this value (and within the "octave" $\flat$ to $\flat$), forming an exact analogy to Pythagorean F and G (in the scale of C) which are symmetrically placed around equal-tempered F♯ (and within the octave C to c).

The durations listed in the table may also, of course, be presented graphically, and for a number of reasons a logarithmic scale is best suited to such a presentation. (The value of each duration in "cents"—the logarithmic unit most familiar to musicians—has been listed.) In Ex. 1 a slide rule is illustrated, the scales of which have been plotted in this manner, with note values presented on the two slides and metronome calibrations (and durations in seconds) on the fixed faces. The setting of

closest to x, whether it is larger or smaller. In the case of 3,6,12, etc., which are equally placed between powers of two, the "older" rule is of course applied. The "logic" of this method is just as sound as that of the "older" rule, and the resulting visual image is probably more musical and easier to read. Unfortunately, the illustrations for this article were prepared before the publication of Carter's "Letter." As for the abbreviation of artificial divisions in triple and compound meters, the Carter-Miquelle approach, though it tends to a proliferation of dots, appears distinctly superior to the method described by Hindemith, both for the reasons given in his letter and because it avoids the introduction of ambiguity in out-of-context citations.

[11] A truly excellent percussionist, who is experienced in the performance of the most intricate contemporary music, recently failed repeatedly to read the following figure as a series of nine equal notes:

the slides illustrates the common tempo ratio 3:4, as for example in the following tempo shift: ♪ = 108; ←♪ = ⌐3→; ♩ = 72. In Ex. 2, a more elaborate form of the same device illustrates the unusual ratio 14:15; a subtle rhythmic modulation involving this ratio occurs in Carter's Double Concerto, m. 105: ♩ = 105 (♩. = 70); ←♩♪ = ⌐5→; ♩ = 98. Simple calculations relating note values, tempi and durations (of individual events, sections or compositions), especially if the data and required information are approximations, may often be accomplished more quickly with such devices than by mental arithmetic. The discovery of note-value equivalents, or near equivalents, in two given tempi is particularly convenient.

The term "irrational" is sometimes used to designate bracketed note values. This is unfortunate and misleading, because all conventional (including bracketed) durations are rational fractions (in the mathematical sense of the word) of the unit duration, which is a function of tempo. (A better name for the more intricate fractional values is "artificial divisions," but it, too, is unfortunate.)[12] Truly irrational duration relationships are of course conceivable and practical, even in a fixed tempo, but in conventional notation they can be expressed only by using such crude, extraneous devices as the fermata, or the vague instruction "tempo rubato". Truly irrational *tempo* relationships are most frequently encountered in constant slow accelerations, where, if metronomic indications are given, close rational approximations to the intended irrational relationships are generally notated.[13]

In analog notation, however, note values will *in general* be truly irrational, truly incommensurable. The attempt, in practice, to express conventional, rational, proportional, commensurable note values in purely spacial notation systems inevitably leads to gross inaccuracies in performance. If unmodified analog notation is held to be useful at all, it must be assumed that the tolerance for performance error in music which employs chiefly irrational duration and tempo relationships is greater than in rationally proportioned music. This assumption is probably correct in

---

[12] Why is 3/5 more artificial than 3/4? The use of the word "artificial" in this context implies that only binary (and perhaps ternary) divisions are *natural;* this may be true in one sense of conventional *notation* (and hence the quasi-justification of the term), but its acoustic, psychological, or musical truth has only occasionally been asserted and never proven (see Wuorinen, *op. cit.*).

[13] There is a very simple example in Carter's Variations for Orchestra (Variation 6), where the following metronome settings appear on successive measures (under the general instruction "Accel. molto"): ♩ = 80, 96, 115, 139, 166, 201, ♩. = ♩ = 80 etc.; the ratios between adjacent numbers approximate $\sqrt[6]{3}$. An equal-tempered tempo scale is notated, as a means of suggesting a steady tempo glissando. Points representing such a series of tempi would of course be equally spaced on the logarithmic metronome scales of Exx. 1 and 2. More complex and subtler applications of the same approach to tempo relationships—an approach which is complementary and antithetical to "metric modulation"—are not uncommon in Carter's recent music; see, for example, the Second Quartet, p. 55.

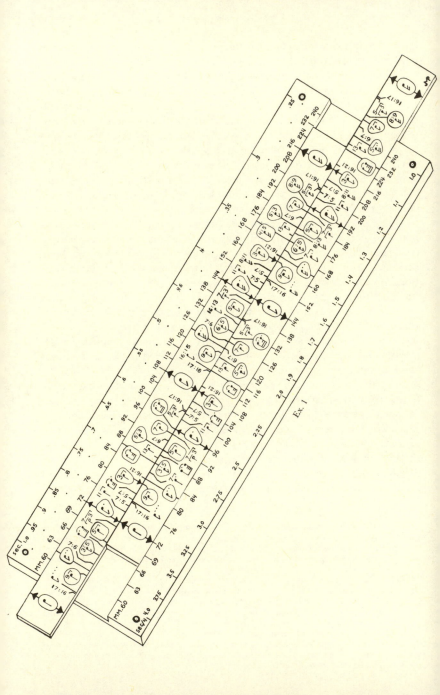

Ex. 1

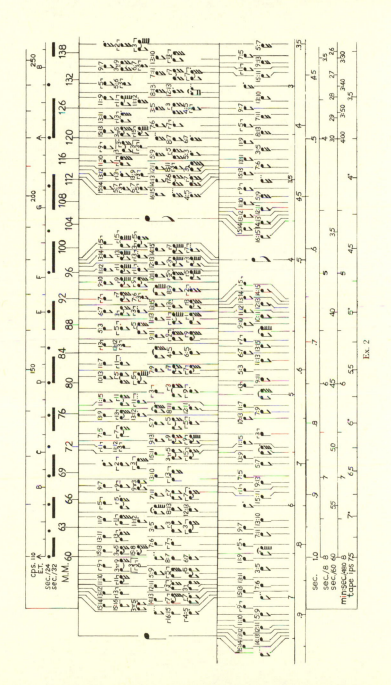

Ex. 2

many cases. Several compromise notations have of course been developed and applied in an effort to derive the benefits of both analog and conventional systems, and, although none of these notations has as yet attracted a significant number of composers, there is no doubt that the best of them offer unprecedented flexibility and versatility.

The capacity to express irrational duration relationships directly and simply is not in itself the chief virtue of analog notations. Any irrational note value can be approximated by one of the conventional values listed in the above table, with an error that is almost certainly tolerable musically, and very probably below the threshold of perceptibility, in most tempi. On the other hand, conventional notation does in practice impose substantial limitations on the variety of feasible *patterns* of duration, and these limitations may be wholly circumvented by recourse to analog notation.

One simple example should illustrate what is meant. The following pitch-duration pattern poses no notational problems:

Ex. 3

A semitone transposition of this presentation of a twelve-tone series results in a permutation or scrambling of its pitches:

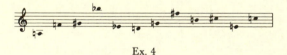

Ex. 4

If the duration values of the original pattern were to be scrambled in the same way (so that each pitch in the transposition would be associated with the same duration as in the original pattern), the resulting series of durations would be exceedingly difficult to present in conventional notation:[14]

[14] This is not suggested as an interesting variation technique, for compositional application! The device of transposition is mentioned solely to provide an impersonal basis for permutation of a series of durations, something which itself is interesting not as a musical resource but as a theoretical possibility or tool. Objections to a duration basis for rhythmic serialization are strongly voiced in Milton Babbitt, "Twelve Tone Rhythmic Structure and the Electronic Medium," PERSPECTIVES OF NEW MUSIC, Fall 1962, pp. 49–79. Essentially, such a basis will fail because of the absence in the realm of duration of any phenomenon analogous to octave equivalence in the realm of pitch, and the absence of durational equal-temperament. Conventional rhythm notation, with its binary divisions, suggests an octave equivalence of duration which simply does not correspond to a perceptual reality comparable to the pitch octave (which, strangely, is not at all reflected in staff notation).

Analog notation could convey to a human performer this new pattern as easily as the original one, and with as little precision.

The pattern-limitations of conventional notation are complex and subtle. Their detailed definition, and a study of the ways in which composers in the past have attacked and overcome them, might prove rewarding and valuable. The fact that many composers who employ conventional notation in writing for conventional (non-electronic) media are not acutely and constantly aware of their existence may be due to the educational process: we are conditioned to think in terms of musical patterns which are not very difficult or awkward to express in conventional notation. Blind submission to such conditioning is not necessarily conducive to the conception of vital rhythmic ideas: we have the witness of Stravinsky to the fact that the *Danse Sacrale* was conceived, and played on the piano, before it could be notated. But analog notation, for all its easy attractions, is not the only available escape from those limitations which remain in modern conventional notation, and it entails sacrifices many are unwilling to make. To use Ben Johnston's terminology, insofar as analog notation implies a musical organization based solely upon a linear (interval) scale of duration, it denies those higher levels of organization based upon a proportional (ratio) scale, and the result may be a loss of integrative power and intelligibility.[15] Further extensions of rational notation are possible which may eventually cancel all pattern limitations, or reduce them to insignificance. The music of Babbitt, Carter and Shapey, to name only three dissimilar Americans, point in this direction.

1965

[15] Johnston, *op. cit.*, p. 60.

WHAT INDETERMINATE
NOTATION DETERMINES

DAVID BEHRMAN

TRADITIONAL notation has been abandoned in so much of the last decade's music that players are no longer shocked by the prospect of tackling a new set of rules and symbols every time they approach a new composition. Learning a new piece can be like learning a new game or a new grammar, and first rehearsals are often taken up by discussions about the rules—about "how" to play rather than "how well" (which must be put off until later).

The traditional role of notation was to fix certain elements of performance while leaving others to the "musicianship" passed on to a player by his teachers and absorbed from his environment. Many of the things done by the musician, and absolutely essential to good performance, were not to be found in the score: deviation from the metric values, differentiation in timbre and intonation, types of pedalling and tonguing and sliding, as well as aspects of the sort described by a vague word or two—"con fuoco," "lebhaft"—words so vague they had meaning only to a player culturally conditioned to them.

It was taken for granted that any performer could obey the notation's literal demands. Whether he was talented or not depended upon whether his "musicianship" could "breathe life" into the music.

In the course of at least one branch of development of serial music, the performer's "musicianship" came to outlive its usefulness. The composer no longer expected him to read between the lines of his score. Deviation from the notated rhythms was not desirable in a style in which the periodic beat of the meter was no longer felt to pulsate beneath the rhythm of the sounds superimposed upon it. Deviation in intonation, dynamics, timbre, etc., would merely obscure the structures extended to cover each of those parameters. So the player of this sort of music had less to do than he had formerly: his job was now to obey the literal requirements of the score in a deadpan fashion. To make up for the suppression of interpretation, the specifications grew more numerous and exacting than ever before. The degree of precision demanded was sometimes so high that it taxed the ability of the performer and led him to deliver what in fact was a subjective interpretation—to play in a way that would "sound as though" he were fulfilling the notation's demands.

Some of the musicians who went through the experience of "total organization" have described the lessons that they thought might be learned from it. It became apparent that the range of sound which a player is capable of covering is so extensive and so susceptible to nuance that no notation can hope to control the whole of it, especially not at once. In such a view the composer, with his rules and his notation, is in a position comparable to the dramatist's, with his stage directions and his dialogue. Both score and script are at the mercy of the interpreter who can make a thousand realizations of every symbol, whether of a noise, a note, or a word. The more a composer tries to control, the larger the number of elements over which the player must distribute his powers of concentration, and the more conventional will be his execution of individual elements—the more will be left to technical reflexes built up in the course of his training. But a "conventional" technique may no longer have an expressive content which the composer wishes to incorporate into his music. His ideal may be to put the player in a fresh frame of mind, to shock him out of an environment which puts a smoke screen of technique between himself and the experience of playing, to make him feel as though the making of sounds on an instrument were a fresh experience. If this is his point of view, then his notation, it was said, ". . . should be directed to a large extent towards the people who read it, rather than towards the sounds they will make." [1]

Examples of three new notations by two composers are discussed below. The examples were chosen from among works recently recorded (by Columbia Records and Time Records). Each is followed by a transcription, in conventional metric notation, of the fragment's realization on a record. The purpose was to show the relationship between a new notation and its concrete results in performance. Transcriptions were made by transferring the recorded fragments to tape, where pitches and durations could be more easily examined. Distances between attacks and releases of sounds could be measured with a stop watch or ruler.

For the transcriptions of fragments from *Durations 1* and Duet II, the tempo of the stop watch was adopted, with each beat (second) subdivided into two groups of five (10ths of a second). Times were fixed by taking the average stop watch reading after a number of timing trials (made at half-speed). The first sound in each fragment was arbitrarily assigned the

---

[1] Cornelius Cardew, "Notation—Interpretation . . . ," *Tempo* (Summer, 1961), p. 26. Notations carrying this idea the farthest have been made by younger composers. Young, Ichiyanagi, Chiari, and others may provide the player with instructions in written or orally delivered prose; Gordon Mumma's notation, in "Megaton," consists of advice and physical demonstration given to the player by the composer—both before and during performance.

downbeat of the first measure in the transcription. There is, of course, no accentual significance in the relative position of downbeats and upbeats.

Ex. 1, Feldman, *Durations I*

The pieces written in this notation, which looks at first glance like a featureless succession of chords, tend to assume four-part configurations in performance: 1) the opening moments—all instruments attacking simultaneously (a sound which will occur nowhere else, except through extraordinary coincidence); 2) the main body of the piece, during which all players are engaged in moving independently through their parts; 3) the music which occurs after the fastest player has finished, during which the number of players more or less gradually diminishes; 4) the ending solo by the slowest player—which can run from a note to a system or two or more.

In this "race-course" form ("start together, move independently, stop when you reach the finish line"), the consequence to a performer for moving the slowest is to be left stranded, with the shelter of his comrades' sounds removed and his last sounds to play alone.

The proportions of the four "parts" are determined by the degree to which the speeds of the players vary. Speed is fixed neither by the notation itself nor by the rules accompanying it, which specify only that "the duration of each sound is chosen by the performer. All beats are slow." (Whether or not a note has the value of one beat is left unspecified—a conscious omission of the type that has been described as "obliging the player to seek out just such rules as he needs or as will make sense of the notation.") [2] But in practice there are limits concerning the speed appropriate to the notation, and an interpretation exceeding them would be a poor one. The unwritten rules describing such limits may in fact be imposed in rehearsal by the composer, the conductor, or by the players familiar with the composer's work upon those unfamiliar with it. They describe the boundaries of a personalized style (or tradition or "common practice") built up by the composer and passed on in the course of performances to his players. They might be compared to the rules governing those facets of performance, unsettled in the scores of the past, which have become perennial subjects of speculation among musicologists: aspects (such as rhythmic alteration in the Baroque) which were passed on through oral rather than written tradition.

One reason that the notation is not more restrictive is the difficulty of conveying that the average speed of all participants, considered over the whole duration of the piece, should fall roughly within the same scale, so that no player ends with an excessive length of solo, but that the tempo of sounds and stretches should be susceptible of free variation. (The cello, in the transcription below, is playing at half the speed of the violin. The relationships change later in the recording, and the violin's lead is narrowed.) What happens in a good performance is that the players, by listening to one another, reach a broad understanding concerning their over-all rate of movement (a sense of ensemble which has to do in part with the musical background common to composer and players, in part with the nature of what they are playing).

Another reason is that constraining the player with too many or overly binding rules might change his mood, the spirit in which he makes his sounds, and the sounds themselves. [3] Feldman's notation and rules suggest as unobtrusively as possible to the player that he produce a kind of sound which it will be pleasurable to hear mingling freely with those of other players, as he moves from one sound to another at a speed and rhythm of his own choosing. Since the sounds are not playing the role of structural building blocks, the fact that they are being made by certain instruments at a certain dynamic level and are heard together is all that matters. (The composer is not concerned with fixing specifically the combination of pitches and timbres that may be heard at any one moment. Calling this "chance composition" would be like saying that the flavor of bouillabaisse has been left to chance because its chef forgot to fix the

[2] Cardew, "Notation," p. 23.

[3] "Suppose the player to behave as follows: he reads the notation and makes himself a picture of the sound (in his mind—the hypothetically imagined sound). He then attempts to reproduce this picture in sound; he compares it with the picture of the sound he had in his mind beforehand, and he may make a few changes, reducing the most glaring discrepancies, releasing wrong notes quickly, reducing the notes he finds too loud, etc., etc." Cardew, "Notation," p. 23.

order in which its ingredients are eaten.) This lack of constraint results often in the appearance of pitch combinations such as widely spaced octaves, or triads, alongside the intervals characteristic of atonal music (such as the "D-major 6/4 chord" appearing in the transcription as three players happen to attack, simultaneously: the flutist and violinist their fifth note, the cellist his third note):

Ex. 2, Transcription of *Durations I*

What controls are present are of a more general kind. Manifold repetitions of single notes and of two and three note patterns thread their way among shifting pitches:

Ex. 3

In *The Swallows of Salangan,* for instruments and chorus, chromatic pitches intrude at intervals into a texture made up largely of shifting, clustered diatonic pitches. As the players and singers move away from the opening downbeat in a gradually dispersing pack, the chromatic pitches are scattered more and more widely throughout the surrounding diatonic territory. (In performance one may be conscious of nothing more than an increasingly faint, periodic darkening in the sound's bright surface.)

In the same composer's "graph" pieces, the principle of selective control is maintained, but free and fixed elements are reversed. In *Projections* I and IV, *Straits of Magellan,* and *Intersections,* etc., the (relatively) fixed elements are time of occurrence, timbre, number, and dynamics; and the (relatively) free one is pitch. Pitch is fixed only in regard to whether it falls within the high, middle, or low portions of the instrument's range. Boundaries of these ranges are for the player to determine.

Here as before, an argument in favor of leaving an element unspecified is that fixing it would be irrelevant—would not change the flavor of the music, which is already well established. Again, in leaving the player free to make decisions about one element, the composer is directing a psychological measure at him in hopes of making him think twice about what he is doing. As part of his interpretation, the player must ask himself what sort of pitches are most appropriate—in effect, what sort of music it is that he is playing. In a piece of thin texture, such as *Projection IV,* the pitches chosen by each player will be heard individually, and the resulting sound will be a combination of the decisions characteristic of both of them.

The meter of the original notation is retained in this transcription. It should be read conventionally (by assuming that the players furnished with it deviate somewhat from the written time values).

The violinist stresses sevenths and fourths here, and avoids octaves—all this legitimately in the tradition of serial music. But we know from some of his other works that the composer enjoys octaves too: in fact, his notation provides the likelihood of their appearance here as intervals between pitches of the two instruments.

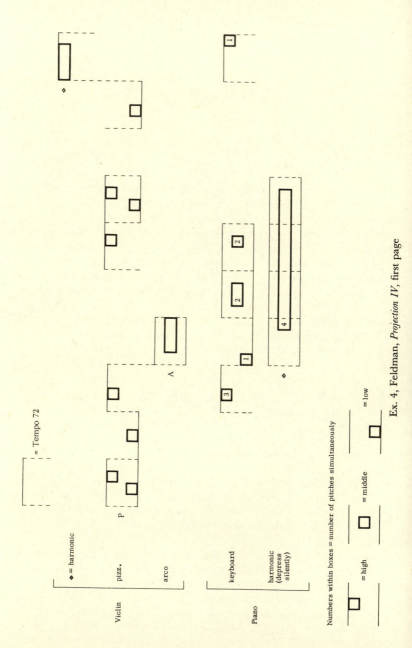

Ex. 4, Feldman, *Projection IV*, first page

Ex. 5, Transcription of *Projection IV*

In the notations discussed above, a single element—pitch or speed—is left almost free of control, while another, dynamic levels in both cases, is confined to one end of its spectrum. Selectivity in control is essential to Christian Wolff's recent notation as well. In his work the relationships among fixed and freed elements and the degree of specification of elements shift about from symbol to symbol. And added to the player's concerns is a novel method of linking what he does, and when, with the sounds he hears being made by other players.

(Duration: ● = 1 second or less; ○ = any; □ = very long to medium.

H (Horn player) — start and stop together

P starts, holds till H sounds; both release together

P plays (short note). H begins short note as P's note ends.

P (Pianist) —

H plays short note. P starts at its end, holds any duration.

3
0

play 3 notes of any duration, together, overlapping, or mute (1) separate. Silence between tones is free. Mute one of them.

* = a noise

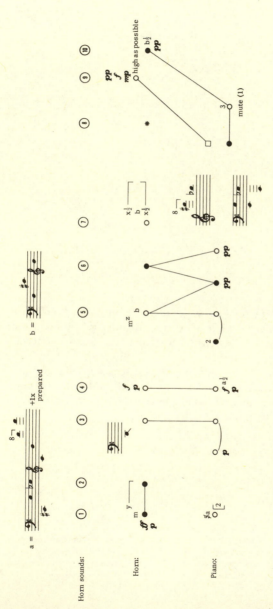

♭ = line means 1) notes must be unequal in some respect (e.g. duration or loudness); 2) notes must be varied each time the section is repeated.

[2 = 2 notes are to be attacked simultaneously.

a½; b½ = transpose any of the tones in the source half a tone higher or lower.

bx½ ⌐ = raise or lower pitches (of source b) half a tone and transpose to any higher octave.

mʸ and mᶻ = two different kinds of mutes or muting (to be chosen by player).

Ex. 6, Christian Wolff, Duet II

This is one of six fragments which make up the score of Duet II, for horn and piano. The order in which the fragments are played, the number of times they may be repeated, and the total duration of performance are free.

In performing the piece, the players follow two sorts of procedures alternately:

1. To begin, and every time a fragment has been completed: the first player to make the next sound determines which fragment is to come next by playing the first sound of that fragment. The other player hears the sound, recognizes the fragment that it begins, and responds by playing his own part in that fragment. Or, he may a) fail to recognize the cue, b) start another fragment himself simultaneously with the first player. In any case, the directions provide that as soon as the players realize that they are not playing the same fragment together, they should break off and "start" over again (follow the procedure just described). Such breakdowns in coordination are a part of the piece and have musical characteristics, in performance, of their own—rhythms and pitch structures, for instance, which have a quality different from the rest of the music.

When the players have come to know the piece well, one may even try to disguise his cues to the other in hopes of confusing him (when a cue's pitch is unspecified, for instance, he may use a pitch belonging to another cue's pitch-source).

2. During the fragments themselves—after one has been "cued in" by one player and responded to by the other—the players have a path to follow, from sound to sound, until they finish the last symbol in the fragment. The time at which a player begins or ends his next sound may be determined by him or by a sound made by the other player. In the latter event, he must wait for the other's sound to occur and then react to it—sometimes as fast as he can—without the benefit of advance warning. (For the horn player, this is the situation at his 6th, 9th, and 10th sounds above.) Here the player's situation might be compared to that of a ping-pong player awaiting his opponent's fast serve: he knows what is coming (the serve) and knows what he must do when it comes (return it); but the details of how and when these things take place are determined only at the moment of their occurrence.

The game-like features just described seem closer in spirit to certain Oriental musical traditions than to those of the West. The disguising of cues is similar to a technique in Indian Music called *Laratgheth*—a cross-rhythm generated by soloist and percussionist when, in competition, each tries to confuse the other with rhythmic patterns played off the strong beat.

In moving from symbol to symbol, the player is required to shift his attention continually from one aspect of what he does to another. Each symbol has its own combination of controls, applied selectively:

$\sqrt{}$ = determined to some extent (fixed, or possibilities narrowed)
P = determined by pianist . . . by way of notation
S = simultaneity (determined by the first to act next)

sounds:	1st	2nd	3rd	4th	5th	6th	7th	8th	9th	10th
pitch			$\sqrt{}$		$\sqrt{}$		$\sqrt{}$		$\sqrt{}$	$\sqrt{}$
timbre	$\sqrt{}$				$\sqrt{}$			$\sqrt{}$		
time of attack				S	$\sqrt{}$	P			P	P
time of release (duration)	$\sqrt{}$	$\sqrt{}$	S	S	S	$\sqrt{}$				
dynamic	$\sqrt{}$	$\sqrt{}$		$\sqrt{}$					$\sqrt{}$	$\sqrt{}$

Horn Part

The degree of control is relative. Where the pitch column is blank, as at the 1st sound, the player must choose any 1 pitch from among the 36 or 40 or more pitches within his range. At the 7th sound, his possibilities are cut down by about half (see below): he must choose one pitch from among the 15 or 16 of the transposed, shifted pitch source which fall within his range. At the 10th sound, he must choose 1 from among 6 pitches; at the 5th, 1 from among 3; only the 3rd sound is fixed (the slanting line means that the D is to be played slightly flat).

The same sort of scale, running from fixed to free, is applied to the other elements as well. The dynamics run (in the horn part) from unspecified, through any selection or combination in any order of three levels (9th note—pp, f, mp) down to fixed (2nd and 10th sounds).

The transcriptions below approximate two realizations of the notation quoted above. They were made from the performance by David Tudor and Howard Hillyer (the fragment happens to occur twice during their six-minute version, on Time Records 58009):

If one were comparing these two fragments and had no access to the original notation, their relationship would surely seem puzzling. The two are obviously the same music—the groupings of sounds, the general continuity, many of the pitches, are the same—but varied seemingly without method, full of small, erratic changes in pitch, configuration, numbers of notes. A glance at the original makes clear that the discrepancies come about through an active use of the indeterminacy linking composition with notation, instrumental technique, and the players' personalities. It is impossible to know, in advance, what specifically will result from a

symbol such as ⦦ (the horn's fourth note). The player here must concentrate at once upon beginning the next sound when he wants to or
playing immediately if the other player beats him to the draw. The same
applies to its time of ending. Since there is no advance warning, there will
be a slight pause between the attacks and releases of initiator and
follower—the time it takes the follower to translate information received
by his ear into mechanical action on his instrument. (The interval between the time a driver sees an unexpected obstacle in the road and his
application of the brakes is comparable.) The attack will have a rushed,
nervous, cramped quality that could not have been notated in any other
way. It is this quality that the composer is concerned with, rather than
with the sounds' other measurements.

What sort of delayed reactions result from this notation may be seen
in both transcriptions: in the lack of simultaneity in releases of horn and
piano at the horn's 3rd, 4th, and 5th notes; and in the pauses separating
the horn's 6th note from its piano neighbors.

A list of operations to be performed by the horn player in making the
fragment's ten sounds would include the following:

SOUNDS

1st and 2nd   1st is short, of any pitch, muted by one of two methods
selected for use in the piece; its dynamic ingredients are
ff and/or p. It is connected, legato, to the 2nd sound: short,
same mute, any pitch, mp.

(In the first transcription there is a pause between the
1st and 2nd horn sounds. Perhaps the horn player was
unsure about whether the pianist had begun the same fragment that he had, broke off, reassured himself about the
pianist's activity, and went on to his second note.)

3rd   Horn player waits for pianist's next sound which may
come very quickly after the first group of five or after any
length of silence; plays his 3rd sound (a slightly flat D_2 at
any dynamic, without muting, beginning any time after
the piano note's attack but before its release or fadeout;
the two players release simultaneously (cut-off is determined by the first player to act next).

4th   (After a pause of any duration): any pitch, any duration,
dynamic ingredients f and/or p, begun and ended together
with the next sound of the pianist. (Horn is the initiator in
both transcriptions.)

DAVID BEHRMAN

Ex. 7A, Transcriptions of Duet II

Ex. 7B

5th   Played a short time after the pianist's next two attacks
             (which may be overlapping, simultaneous, or separated by
             any amount of silence); using one of the three pitches
             given; at any dynamic; with the second kind of muting;
             released simultaneously with the end of the pianist's
             second sound.

6th   Any dynamic, any pitch, duration short; begun just as
             pianist's short pp sound is released.

7th   Beginning, duration, dynamic free. One pitch is to be
             chosen from among 15 possibilities. (To find the pitch of
             this note the player must raise or lower one of the three
             pitches in Source b a half-step and transpose it any number
             of octaves up or down. It turns out that 15 or 16 of these
             transpositions fall within a horn's range. The player has
             any time in which to jump this small hurdle.)

8th   Any noise (made with the instrument), character and
             dynamics unspecified, played between the attack and
             release of pianist's square note.

9th   Begun when pianist's square note ends; highest pitch
             possible; dynamic ingredients pp and/or f and/or mp;
             duration, otherwise free, may here be determined by the
             context (sound must be broken off in time to play the 10th
             sound).

10th   Short; begun at end of the last of pianist's three sounds;
             dynamic pp; one pitch chosen from among six available.

First transcription: after his 7th note the horn player hears a number of
piano sounds and must decide which ones correspond to which symbols.
Evidently the pianist's low F corresponds to his square symbol and the E
above it to the black, since the E is followed by three sounds (the $^3_0$ symbol)
while the F continues. Piano's releases beyond this point are not audible
on the record. (The horn player may "see" the release of these sounds as
the pianist's hands leave the keyboard; or he may guess about the time
they are released.) Note: the horn's 9th and 10th sounds will appear in
reverse order if the piano's F is held after the D and Eb are released.

Second transcription: The 9th and 10th sounds of the horn seem to come
two or more seconds after the release of the last piano sounds. Such a situation arises often in playing from this notation. Waiting for the release of a
sound—hard to hear if it is a sustaining piano note—one hears other,

louder sounds intervene and then realizes that the original note is no longer sounding. Knowing that one has missed the cut-off cue, one proceeds (tardily) to the next symbol.

The complexities of this notation are directed less at an arrangement of sounds resulting from performers' actions than at the conditions under which their actions are to be produced. (It addresses itself to the player's mind as well as to his fingers). By comparison, even the most complex "totally organized," conventionally written scores seem simple—if considered from the point of view of what the player has to think about (his part tells him which note to play first, how to play it, how long to hold it, how long to wait before playing the second sound, etc., etc., until he has finished). Wolff's notation approaches the role of rules governing the conduct of games. It tends to produce characteristic sound combinations, recognizable as the composer's "signatures," just as a game has its characteristic "moves." (Among them are grace notes jumping back and forth among players, the sudden cut-off of a long sound just after another begins, the thin sustaining sound made by a player who is waiting for his cue and is not sure whether he may have missed it.)

One of the criteria with which to judge a notation is the question of what, if any, the consequences are of playing well or badly (what incentives are there for realizing the notation in the way intended and expressed by the composer). In Wolff's notation, the players must listen with such care to one another that an inaccuracy is liable to alter the signal received by one's partner and so to disturb the continuity. The same is true of the notation used by Feldman in *de Kooning* and *Vertical Thoughts,* in which a chain of sounds links player to player (one is directed to begin playing at the moment when another's sound begins to fade). Elsewhere, Feldman's scores present the player with an "honor system" notation. With no one to check up on what he does, the player's incentive for doing his best is (presumably) the pleasure of contributing to a sound world whose transparency is such that the smallest detail remains perfectly audible within it. Expressed in the notations of both artists is an idea that music must remain a creative activity for players as well as an arrangement of symbols by the composer.

1965

PREPARING STOCKHAUSEN'S
MOMENTE

BROCK MC ELHERAN

In the summer of 1963, Lukas Foss, as music director of the Buffalo Philharmonic Orchestra, invited our college to send a choir to sing the American première of Karlheinz Stockhausen's latest work, *Momente,* to be conducted by the composer and accompanied by thirteen members of the orchestra. At that time, neither the score nor a recording of the work was available. We eventually received a tape, made by the Cologne Radio Chorus and Orchestra, on which we heard a piece with practically no singing, recognizable rhythms or intervals, but rather a conglomeration of claps, shouts, moans, shrieks, bangs, squawks, snaps, and hiccups. The score itself was four feet across, eighteen inches deep and covered with indecipherable markings; the parts were almost as large. Included were some typed instructions and a seating plan showing that there were four widely separated choirs of sixteen singers, four to a part, using two music stands to hold each choral part (as the singers had to use their hands as well as their feet and voices). The instructions consisted entirely of terse details in a sometimes unintelligible word order, including such cryptic phrases as "II, III, IV, repeat text 1½(2) times 12(15) syllables," "A, T, Almost voiceless in throat-to voice-voiceless. B: compressed in throat. At (*): deep "E" if K_1 follows hold it through K_1."

"Each three syllables" (evidently intended to mean "three syllables each").

"Vibrate right hand furiously"

"Shout in confusion; each of the 7 syllables equally often."

There were no page numbers, no rehearsal letters, no movement numbers—only occasional large black letters, usually with an arabic numeral as a subscript. Thus we were unable to find the passages to which the instructions applied. In several places in the score, fragmentary extra pages had been glued into slits. Listening to the tape while following the score was little help, since the movements were in different orders on each, and without being able to read the notation, we couldn't find our place.

But in January 1963, Stockhausen arrived for an American tour, and we decided to meet and work together. As Stockhausen explained his new system of notation, it came to seem clear and logical; in fact, I have since found it actually easier to read and teach than standard notation. In certain places, Stockhausen found it simpler to revert to traditional notation, but after we developed facility in the new system, it was the traditional spots that gave us the most trouble. I shall describe this system as used in *Momente,* elements of which were also introduced earlier in his *Carré.*

The music is read from left to right. Vertical lines running down the full length of the page group the music into its main time groups, comparable to bar lines and measures. At the top of each "bar line" there is a large arabic numeral, giving the number of subdivisions of the "measure." This corresponds to the top digit in traditional time signatures. Thus far, there is little new. But the interesting and novel feature is that the "measure" is divided by shorter vertical lines corresponding to beats. If the beats are to be performed at regular intervals, these "beat-lines" (to coin a term) are regularly spaced; if the beats are irregular, or accelerating or retarding, they are spaced proportionally. The conductor uses standard beat patterns, and the performers must be extremely alert when the beats are unequal. At the bottom of the page, a number written in the middle of each "measure" gives the duration in seconds. The conductor must practice with a stop watch, just as in traditional contemporary music he might use a metronome.

Each performer's part is written between two horizontal lines. Short sounds, such as a shout, a bang, or a staccato note, are written on or between the appropriate beat-lines. A sustained sound stretches from the beat-line on which it commences as far as the composer wants. Exact pitches, if required, are shown on a staff; variable pitches are indicated by writing relatively higher or lower in the space. Standard musical marks for dynamics, accents, etc. are used as required. New musical sounds, or sounds not usually used in concert music, need explanation and in many cases an aural demonstration.

In the score there was little explanation and no legend, something which will be remedied in future printings. Stockhausen, like Bach, thought that he alone would perform the work, and in Cologne he explained each symbol as he went along. He now finds that others can learn the techniques with a little help, and that his music can be performed without his physical presence.

I extracted a list of symbols from the score and started work by handing them out to the singers, asking that they be memorized before the first rehearsal. Some of those used most frequently are:

)L	African tongue click
)F	snap fingers
)E	combine the above

F	stamp foot
F - - - - - -	shuffle feet continuously
S	speak syllable from the memorized text
S ⁀⁀	sustain a syllable; approximate pitch shown (gliss.)
Hu--------	voiceless coughing
Я 〜〜	sustain a uvular "R," voiced or voiceless as indicated
H	single hand clap
H - - - - - -	continuous clapping
H〜〜	rub hands together
K	hit knee

One part might read as follows (for tenors of Choir IV):

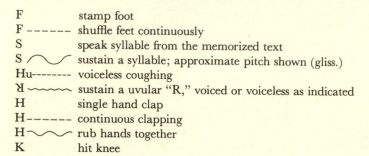

Ex. 1

This indicates a loud clap on the second beat of an irregular seven measure (which takes 10 seconds to play), a shouted syllable on the 5th beat, a quiet finger snap on 7; then a sustained syllable, starting high, on 1 of the next measure sliding down, cresc.-dim., and turning upwards slightly on 2, cutting off on 1 of the next measure, which comes very suddenly; then clapping, f dim. p, from beat 2 to 3, with a loud shout, clap and foot stamp on beat 4. The last measure lasts 5 seconds and the beats are regular.

Here is an example of combined Stockhausen and staff notation:

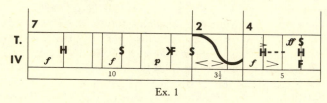

Ex. 2

Notice how easy it is to see what beat the note ends on, and where to put the final consonant. The notes grouped

Ex. 3

are to be performed as quickly as possible, like grace notes, in this case starting on beat 1.

Stockhausen uses International Phonetics in many cases, sometimes for actual German words and sometimes to indicate meaningless sounds.

One wishes all foreign languages were written this way in choral music. A little practice in the system helps a singer pronounce any European language without learning endless rules and exceptions.

The notation for the two Hammond organs, eight brass instruments, and three percussionists follows the same system. Staves are usually used for the organs and brass, with symbols for three different brass mutes. One passage for the electronic organs is particularly striking. Over a period of several minutes, each player is required to hold his left hand down on all the notes of a chromatic scale, sliding it very slowly the length of the keyboard. Above the staves, a graph shows the composer's suggestions for altering the tone by increasing or decreasing the higher and lower harmonics, a capability of Hammond organs largely ignored by composers.

Several times the composer wants the percussionist to scratch on the surface of an instrument, as though he were writing. This produces a sound which comes in irregular waves, like distant thunder. He indicates this by a wavy line resembling handwriting, and is very insistent that the performers follow the loops and scrolls as closely as possible, to produce the pitch and tone changes exactly as specified.

A frequent device of Stockhausen's is to require certain things to be done ad-lib, within a designated time. For example, the singers all had to memorize a passage from the Song of Solomon, and each one of the sixty-four was assigned a different syllable to start on. Thus when the part said "S" for all singers, each one said his first syllable; at the next "S" he said his next one, and so on; this guaranteed a dense mixture of different vowels and consonants, with no one sound being heard separately, when properly balanced and blended. At other times the singers would have to speak, over a period of eleven seconds, five syllables irregularly spaced, but more or less evenly distributed—that is, not bunched all at one end. Our first tendency was to say them all too soon; we found that seconds are much longer than we thought. It was only when we began to sense how long eleven seconds actually lasts that we could space our syllables or notes properly, and the audience would hear the proper dappled, irregular sounds.

The same technique, called "statistical music," is also frequently used for instrumental notes. It enables the composer to achieve great rhythmic variety without notating beats divided to many decimal points and therefore impossible to reproduce the same way every time. Stockhausen says "you don't have to count all the leaves on a tree to enjoy foliage, and certain leaves could be rearranged or interchanged without destroying the general effect." Although such passages would never be performed twice the same way, they would sound the same. A traditional unmeasured trill in a string section or tremolo exhibits the same principle.

One of the most unusual passages was one for two sopranos and two altos striking tambourines. This was written on four lines, with an "X" for each note, spaced proportionately within large time units. A zigzag line showed what might be called the firing order. Only the first note of each unit could be conducted, as the conductor had too many other things to attend to. The performers played partly by sensing the elapsed time, partly by listening to each other.

Many other details in the score occurred only once and required much explanation and demonstration. In one short passage, sixteen soloists each performed a series of different noises, and then traded around and did three of their colleagues' sounds. One of these included a trilled "r," at a moderate pitch, falsetto, with pitch wavering slightly at irregular intervals. Another was a series of irregular grunts—mouth closed, pitch rising and falling widely in irregular loops (indicated), and opening at specified points to the vowel "ɔ" (International Phonetics)—taking six seconds. Most of the sixteen sounds could not be described so simply. Each had its own diagram, and frequently, its own descriptive phrase.

Momente is a collection of "Moments," like Schubert's *Moments Musicaux*. Like a collection of Romantic piano pieces, it is a series of unrelated movements written in a free, improvisational form. There is, however, one important difference. Stockhausen expects the performer to vary the order of movements at will, and even provides for passages from one movement to be inserted into its neighbors. For each concert the score may be rearranged, in accordance with certain instructions; the extracts or "inserts" may be glued into certain slits in the score, and their duration and volume are varied depending on the context, as indicated by a long list of rules on each sheet. Then the parts are prepared in whatever order has been selected for the particular concert.

The pages thus cannot be numbered permanently, and the complex combinations of letters and subscript numbers refer to the different "Moments." The composer alone understands the principles behind the rules and the numbers, and he has not had time to write all these down or explain them. (He says it is very complicated.) At one point when we were working on the score, he became confused and spent fully half an hour trying to understand his own instructions concerning the omission of inserts when a certain section was repeated. I suggested he make up a new rule for the occasion, but he preferred to pore over his notations on the score until he was able to decode them. This was the only evidence I ever saw of rigidity in his ideas. In all other matters he seemed highly flexible and willing to make alterations in the interest of practicality.

In addition to making vocal, hand and foot noises, the choir in *Momente* is required to play simple instruments. The composer gave me samples of the types he wanted, and we spent much time trying to duplicate them.

Choir I had four tambourines without rattles, and eight long drums made of cardboard tubes. These were tuned to a diatonic scale, not for playing set melodies or chords, but to give a cluster of pitches rather than one note. Choir II had twelve pairs of claves, selected for variety of pitch; Choir III presented more of a problem. They had a collection of plastic dishes filled with BB shot. This took endless testing in supermarkets and dime stores to select the right pitches. Mostly they were refrigerator dishes, but for higher notes we used toothbrush cases. The great problem in Choir III was to prevent little trickles of sound after the note; soon they became expert at damping.

Choir IV were the heavyweights, with twenty-four bars of cold rolled steel. Stockhausen had specified car wrenches, but American car wrenches are not only very expensive but are highly unmusical compared with the composer's German pair. This crisis was resolved by rummaging for four hours on the floor of an old blacksmith's shop, testing tone until one's ears rang. Big wads of plastic foam on which to rest the instruments when not in use completed our paraphernalia.

Thus equipped, we met for our first rehearsal. My main concern was the possibility of hostility towards the music. I felt that if the students could take a historical approach and see themselves as the spearhead of a new and exciting movement we could overcome the technical problems. The intense interest of some of the young musicians had convinced me of that, and the results more than justified my confidence.

1965

NOTATION—MATERIAL AND FORM

ROMAN HAUBENSTOCK-RAMATI

W HENEVER WE SPEAK of musical notation, we are talking about the creation of music in the sense of composition, as opposed to improvisation, which views the only real musical creation in music's spontaneous performance. Whether the former represents the developed state and the latter the primitive state of the same material—which one is inclined to believe in our Western culture out of a certain indolence—is no longer asserted in all quarters with the same certainty.

It is clear that from the point of view of improvisation, notation is considered an unnecessary, interfering factor, or conceded only as an expedient, a means of inspiration or of stimulation. It is regarded as a factor which is interposed between the spontaneous musical idea and its immediate translation into sound. The personality of the improviser, his whole conscious and subconscious being, assumes the dominant role. His spontaneity is freed from the restraints of the notational system. It can be said, therefore, that the music whose ideal is improvisation will be a music that is free of system, and that insofar as that music is written down, it makes use of a free and ambiguous manner of notation and considers this notation as an expedient and as a means of stimulation.

On the other hand, composed music is necessarily bound by system—that is, it must be invented by means of a priori thought, the *sine qua non* for all invention. This then is the music which we Westerners—with or without justification—wish to consider or acknowledge as art.

To recapitulate, improvisation is the natural and spontaneous product of an emotional condition, a product which is bound in time by the length of the improvisation; while a composition is the product of thought, a product of reflection without limit of time. (A composition exists and has meaning even though not played.)

It is just these systematic characteristics of musical notation which demand a priori decisions and logical procedure, these characteristics which make the highly developed art of musical composition possible. From the foregoing it is clear then that the whole history of the development (*development means modification*) of music as art is simultaneously the history of the changing of musical notation. It is clear that the act of composing, which is, as it were, the invention of music, simultaneously entails the invention of a graphic representation of the kind which mirrors the composer's intentions and which makes recognizable the musical idea of the work, not in a literary sense but in the sense of a priori procedure that communicates itself, not in a semantic sense but in the sense of the work's reproducibility. This reproducibility has nothing to do either with the unequivocal nature of the rendition or with the variability of the length of performance time. It applies to all stable and unstable forms alike. The communicability or capacity for being communicated, whose basis is the act of writing down, the notation, is a special kind of communication, a many-layered, complicated process which is based on the simultaneous functioning of several of our senses. It is a process which varies accordingly from individual to individual, but which can be nonetheless reduced to a common denominator.

This common denominator is the correlation between eye, ear, and mechanism or technique. The word "mechanism," as applied here, designates the technique of playing and the technique of composition (including the quality of the handwriting) as well as the medium that is used and the control of that medium.

Our whole musical education strives towards the greatest possible development of these correlatives, a development which can be brought to the point that one element of the eye-ear-mechanism triangle is carried over and translated into another.

I am personally astounded that even today one does not *play* Kandinsky or Miro, even though it would be so simple and easy to do so. Yet even if this does not happen, its possibility proves to me that the decisive moment to confirm or exclude the functioning of this triangle lies in the presence or absence of the musical idea, of the musical intention of each work. The following situation applies for composers:

$$\text{Idea} \rightleftharpoons \text{Eye} \quad \text{Ear}$$
$$\text{Mechanism}$$

Eye-Ear-Mechanism = Composition, act of writing down.

During the compositional process a reciprocal relationship develops between the idea (thought) and the slowly evolving manner of writing it down. This relationship of continuous mutual influence lasts during the whole time of composition, and has the effect that, if the original idea of the work is musically pure and true, the resulting piece will be the best possible in terms of both music and its notation. If I have correctly understood the true origin of a work of music, I am affirming the existence of certain types of musical graphics. For this reason, I organized the first exhibition of this music at Donaueschingen in 1959.

I also affirm it as something new since in principle, if a minimum of good taste is present, I affirm and support all that is new in every art. I do feel that, at least as things now stand, the subject of musical graphics is taken too lightly and accepted too directly from the cliché-like ideas that we owe to the development of our eye-ear relationship. It is produced somewhat too easily. That is the mistake which, I hope, musical graphics will still overcome. There is one thing that cannot be foisted upon it: it makes no pretense to be anything but what it is, a kind of agitation, stimulation, a provocation to improvisation that has again brought to life in our time something musically true and unique. Musical graphics in its most varied forms, from complete graphic representations to brief graphic structures which are interjected into a conventionally notated composition, has influenced the whole of new music with respect to sonorous material, and has obviously enriched it. For that reason one can even excuse much of the totally graphic music, if it is refined, sensitive, and attractive.

There are two motives which are always responsible for a change in the established method of notation: the one I should like to designate as the motive of *discovery,* the other as the motive of *invention.* We relate the notion "discovery" to the material, the notion "invention" to the form. If we keep these two notions separate, it is not to create the impression that a dualism exists between form and material, for we believe that only the organically correct working out of the material makes the construction of musical form at all possible.

The following definition is intended to clarify these issues: *form can only be invented; material can only be discovered.* The transformation of material into form, beginning with the smallest micro-structure and attaining to the final phase of the macro-structure, is a continuous act of transformation from the *discovered into the invented.* This is the only interpretation which makes comprehensible and genuine the unity of the material and the form resulting from it. Only in this manner can the creative role of the imagination be understood as the power which raises the discovered to the realm of the invented.

The enormous scientific and technical progress of recent years, the invention of astounding pieces of equipment in the sphere of electronics and electro-acoustics has led to the discovery of new possibilities in the area of acoustics. This newly discovered universe of acoustic phenomena, which previously could not even be imagined, encompasses an enormous spectrum of sounds and noises. Its creation and technical handling, and the possibility of composing directly on magnetic tapes has fascinated composers and has influenced the development of music and the whole direction of musical thought. The discovery of these new possibilities resulted in inventions of two new species that have moved in two different directions: on the one hand, electronic music, on the other, *musique concrète*. Subsequently they have been combined with each other and with the conventional musical media. The resulting notational problems are of such a magnitude that till now the beginnings of notational solutions have been found only to a quite limited degree.

The small number of existing scores and graphic representations of these kinds of music makes it clear that the possibility of adequate notation depends upon the drastic limitation of the kinds of sounds used and upon their technical handling. The majority of the sound-noise combinations have not yet been graphically fixed in an unambiguous manner, and now the electronic computers are being called upon for assistance. Notation becomes either a kind of literary description or an index of technical data delivered by an electronic computer. In my opinion these methods of notation conceal the danger that in place of an a priori conception of music we have the a posteriori record of a more or less automatically created product, the danger, therefore, of a falsification of the whole a priori character of musical composition. This falsification need not be intentional; it is simply called into being by the machine! This is one of the main reasons why composers have turned once more to an instrumental and vocal music that had been considered dead: in order now, after having been at first completely fascinated by the sounds newly discovered and invented in the electronic studios, to reinvent these new sounds through the means of instrumental and vocal music.

All this has led to an unforeseen enrichment of music and, quite naturally, to a notationally new representation of these new achievements.

The use of magnetic tapes, measured in centimeters per second, led to the graphic representation even of traditionally notated musical events, according to the principle *time equals space*. Consequently, not only the music which was previously restrained by the intermediary role of metric division, but analogously also its notation in score has received the new time-space dimension.

This led logically to the invention of the notation of "proportional meters." This step must in itself be regarded as a victory over the metrical constraint that is an integral part of traditional musical notation. This does not mean, however, that traditional musical notation will be generally repudiated.

But the composer who works with a new and specific situation that is applicable only for a given piece or given musical structure will be repeatedly forced to decide whether to choose means of notation that are traditional or already known, or to invent others in order to convey the new musical situation he desires and intends.

A long series of decisions will be necessary—decisions on how to come to terms with the space-time relationship, on which aspects of traditional notation can be left as they are, and on what must be added or renewed. In a number of cases this may go so far as to force a decision in advance on the kind and size of paper to be used, on whether it should be with or without staff lines, in book form or in the form of loose leaves or of unbroken rolls.

All this means that the achievement of a stationary situation (which, in my opinion, always means the standardization of ideas and the acceptance of a number of established means, and as a result, a falling off of the creative powers) is not yet in sight, simply because of the continually necessary contemplation of the whole situation and the perpetually necessary invention of new means for each new piece of new music. Thus, we are now in a period of permanent renewal.

Earlier we mentioned the existence of a second motive for change: the motive of invention and, therefore, of form.

Just as in three-dimensional painting all means serve the single purpose of bringing everything under a common denominator in the manner of a "frozen surface," so are all notational means of traditional music mobilized to enrich this single perspective, to preserve it and make it stable. All these classic-stable forms are based on the principle of repetition. Since we call every such form based on repetition a "closed form," we can say that all such forms are "stable-closed forms."

In opposition to this principle and through a new use of this principle of repetition, new music developed either so-called "open" or "dynamically closed" forms. They can be stable or variable. The "open" form is from beginning to end a ceaseless flow of continually new events, the exposition of perpetually new structures. "Open form" can be stable or variable. The "dynamically closed form," as it was crystallized in my *Mobile für Shakespeare,* integrates repetition and gives new meaning at the same time to repetition as well as to variation. It is a variable and mobile form which can be designated as "constant variation by means of repetition." All these new forms and their compounds are more or less concerned with the variability of musical material. The real complication of musical notation begins in the moment of transition from the stable forms that are based on unambiguous notation to variable forms that at least in part must be based on an ambiguous notation.

Here lies the point from which all our notational problems and the resulting troubles arise. Stable music, like finely focused photography, has no reason to fall into conflict with the lack of ambiguity in its notation. The situation is different, however, with the variables in the blurred outlines of the musical structures which, as in hazily focused photography or in the photography of a moving object, consider time a co-creating factor. These are two different spheres. The one, which acknowledges that it favors sharply focused photography, should do so, but ought not to make the rules for areas outside its interests, since the fulfillment of its demands would destroy the other area. It is also unfair and misleading, for example, to criticize action photographs from the standpoint of the sharpness of detail. Is there, one often asks oneself, a misunderstanding or an intentional intolerance that takes on different forms in different times?

It is clear that every variable form is unique. Each new composition brings, therefore, new notational problems from the material as well as from the form. Each new composition produces another new struggle between the idea born in the imagination and the material dependent upon the realities of the system and upon technique.

[Translated by Katharine M. Freeman]

1965

NOTATION IN GENERAL—
ARTICULATION IN PARTICULAR

DONALD MARTINO

To all of us whose concern is that delicate process by which sound is translated into symbol and back into sound again, the need to clarify and standardize the existing symbols of our notation must surely be evident. For at a time when performance cannot always be supervised by the composer; when sufficient rehearsal is economically unfeasible; when a real rapport between performer and composer is with rare exception a historical memory; when so many present and past performance traditions exist—within each of which there seems to be so much confusion and ignorance; and when there exist so many compositional attitudes, past and present, within the latter of which the symbologies associated with those many performance traditions are indiscriminately mixed and applied—at such a time our responsibility with respect to notation is greater than it has ever been.

Here is a sample of the results that are to be expected from the specification:

The dash, to performer one (a string player) is a bowing indication whose attack characteristics might range from relatively incisive to barely audible; to performer two (a wind player) it means a soft attack. Performer three reads this sign as tenuto: a term which is variously interpreted as "hold the note its full value" or "hold the note a bit longer than its full value." Attack for this player has never been of great concern. To performer four, a dash means that the note is somehow invested with great expressive significance and, therefore, he is free to play in whatever manner seems most appropriate. And to performers five through infinity it means things the aural results of which are too horrible to contemplate.

For these performers the durational result could range from a dotted eighth-note to a dotted quarter-note: the dynamic result could be crescendo-piano-diminuendo, piano-crescendo-mezzopiano-diminuendo, piano-diminuendo, piano-crescendo, or piano sempre.

If we combine and permute these results, we see that our symbology permits many more interpretations than are compatible with a given musical purpose. The problem is further complicated by the existence for each interpretation of some composer, not necessarily *the* composer, whose intention would thereby have been satisfied.

To some extent, the present confusion surrounding notation and its interpretation can be attributed to the inadequacy, the fallibility, and, in some quarters, the irresponsibility (inadvertent, one hopes) not only of performers but of composers in their proper roles as well as in their secondary roles as educators. It is lamentable that the rudiments of music are almost everywhere neglected in our teaching. For with the proper preliminary training, harmony and counterpoint courses as we know them today would be virtually unnecessary. Music educators would far better serve their cause by introducing the very small child to music through ear training and its attendant disciplines, and by continuing this program as a necessary adjunct to later instrumental studies, than by waiting until he is a near-mature-virtuoso-tonette-player to explain to him what he should hear if only he had been trained to hear it. By then it is probably too late. But even if it were not too late, college administrations would certainly regard such disciplines as highly inappropriate, the faculties would rightly concur, and in any case everyone concerned would long since have lost his tolerance for games that so obviously lack sophistication. Moreover, when such courses do exist they usually contain pitch and rhythm drills that are insufficient even to the proper understanding of traditional music.

As a result of these sins of educational omission, students intellectually capable of speculation at a very high level about matters whose fundamentals they have not yet investigated, are quite common on college campuses. Needless to say, some of these people become professors of forestry, presidents of symphony boards, critics (!), teachers of music, eminent performers or composers, and even tsars of the publishing and recording industries. (Space does not permit the inclusion of all categories.) Each of us in his own way helps to shape the grotesque course of twentieth-century musical history.

And what about manuscript writing and the subtleties of editorial practice? These things are never taught! Notation not being part of our formal education, composers are untrained in editorial procedures.

Since in contemporary America most of the significant young composers are unpublished, these procedures are all the more necessary. Therefore, not only is it possible that a composer might omit a crucial marking, but it is probable that his understanding of the marking if he were to apply it would be so specialized as not to be communicative or at least to be only falsely so.

(For this composer, the peripheral activities to which every year he is more overwhelmingly committed, such as the autographing, editing, publicizing and disseminating of his scores and parts, would require the full-time assistance of his astral double if only he had been trained to project him.)

The ideal musical notation would exactly convey to the performer (i.e., any competent reader of the score) the composer's intention, however precise that intention might have been. While it should be assumed that the composer's notation is as accurate as he is capable or desirous of making it, it does not follow that his notation corresponds exactly to his intention. This paradox may be attributed in many ways to many things, and should we here pursue it, our discussion would become immensely complex.

At present one group of composers insists that the performer's responsibility is the mechanistic reproduction of the manuscript; another faction tells us to re-create in a very personal way; and in some cases, as though we did not have enough to do, we must compose their music for them.

In my own music I attempt as best I can to notate all necessary nuances—but a mechanistic reproduction is furthest from my mind! For instance, my notation

indicates that I am capable of notating (or willing to notate) what I hear, at least to this degree of accuracy. Perhaps some other composer has the skill or the need to notate more precisely:

or

Whatever the degree of accuracy required, it is the composer's responsibility to be as specific as possible; and it is the performer's responsibility—at least initially—to be as faithful to that notation as his faculties permit.

If I take great care with notation, I do not destroy musical expression; I reveal to the performer the kind of musical expression that I intend. And if, thereby, the performer's role as translator is somewhat preempted, the result need not be more mechanistic. If, furthermore, as a consequence of my precision, the performer is made to feel like an automaton, let him practice the new techniques until they are as natural to him as the most fundamental technique on his instrument. In fact, to a competent player, the only new aspect of the problem will in most instances be that he is now required to perform a known technique at a given moment.

Any discussion of symbology must expect to include the notion of license among its definitions of interpretation. Under present circumstances of notation, I for one am perfectly willing to admit that composer's markings must often be altered. But there is a very great difference between purposeful alteration in order to achieve that musical result which every bit of evidence seems to support, and an inadvertent alteration resulting from sloppiness.

Contrary to legend, the composer—even the very great composer at the supreme instant of divine guidance—is fallible. He may at the moment of composition be unaware of the need for additional nuances; but no one will ever know whether these are necessary if performers are unable or unwilling to carry out his instructions. Nevertheless I know of no music past or present which, by my performance standards, is really successful without some creative, interpretive license. But here we are dealing with a very fragile issue: the degree of license that is appropriate in a given instance. Some schools of composition today insist that performers are to play no more (they probably mean no less) than that which is notated. But even in those rare instances when performers nearly attain this surprising goal, these same composers are not satisfied.

When composer X tells us that his music is to be played very precisely, and then takes much liberty in his own performance of it, I suspect that his error is to be sought not in his composition, nor in his performance, but in his translation of musical thought into the medium of words. Even if composer X were to say what he means (and mean what he says), it is a mistake to assume that he speaks for all music of his age; and it is an even greater mistake to infer from his statements some basic law applicable to all composers of

all periods everywhere. Each composer properly belongs somewhere along the continuum bounded at one extreme by total
organization and at the other by chaos. It is the function of the
interpreter to determine at which point or points along this continuum, at moment Y, in the life of composer X, the particular
composition exists. And in every case the best evidence is not what
any composer (critic, biographer, or self-appointed spokesman for a
generation) has said or written in public, but the music itself, in
conjunction with such remarks as the composer may have made
during rehearsal.

We shall not be able to determine whether a resolution of this
conflict between symbology and its interpretation is possible until we
have postulated more precise definitions of the terms and have tested
the results. Meanwhile, whether in one camp the necessary addition
by the performer is called involvement, and is minimal, or at the
other end of the spectrum it is maximal and is termed expressive
license, interpretation, or even creation—we are in every case dealing
merely with different degrees of the same principle.

Although with any notation some license may always be necessary
or desirable, in domains such as articulation, at least, the specification
can be made to whatever degree of accuracy is required. Before
attempting to redefine articulative marks, I will review their present
meanings:

Staccato means detached; the degree or method of detachment is not
specified. And thus, since a single note is automatically detached from
its neighbors, one might logically infer that the staccato dot would be
necessary only when two or more notes occur in sequence—and that it
would be unnecessary on the last note of the sequence:

$$\text{♩̣} \quad \text{♩̣} \quad \text{♩} \quad \text{𝄾}$$

But this sign has come to mean a reduction up to and including three-
quarters of a specified duration:

$$\text{♩̣} = \text{♪ 𝄿·} , \quad \text{♪ 𝄿} , \quad \overset{\overline{\quad 6 \quad}}{\text{♪̣ 𝄿}} , \quad \text{or} \quad \text{♪.. 𝄾} , \text{ etc.}$$

The staccato dot is actually an *informal* durational marking; consequently there is no guarantee that two identically marked notes will be
identically understood. Since detachment automatically produces an
attack, the staccato dot has additionally come to mean a crisp attack,
a crisp decay, or both, or none of these. A rigorous definition of this
symbol would be difficult to construct.

Tenuto means held. The tenuto mark, therefore, would seem to be as redundant as the marking *p sempre* . As a matter of fact, the tenuto mark informally operates on both the duration and the dynamic of a note. Thus, in at least one of its meanings

equals

for which the notation

would logically seem to suffice. But the tenuto mark has also been used to indicate ritenuto—or at least so it is often interpreted:

Berg: Violin Concerto

Furthermore, the dash implies some degree of attack less sharp than the accent mark or the staccato dot; and when used under a slur, it implies an even more subtle attack. Imagine the quandary of that composer who attempts in a single phrase to indicate that each note is to receive a different one of these interpretations:

Some dictionaries make no distinction among the following signs: *sfz*, *sf*, >, ʌ, ˉ . Notes so marked are to be performed with "special stress" or "sudden emphasis." But nowhere is there a statement concerning the method by which sudden emphasis or stress is to be achieved. Nowhere is it explicitly stated that notes marked in this manner are to be "louder than" their neighbors. In practice, the sign > is so interpreted that a change of dynamic results not only between accented and unaccented notes but within an accented note.

are some of the

possible consequences of the following notation:

It is worth remarking that the accent mark did not imply continual diminuendo to Schoenberg, since in m. 51 of the Phantasy, Op. 47, he writes

The circumflex accent ∧, although commonly understood as an intensification of >, is defined as follows by Schoenberg: "Notes marked ∧ should be given a certain degree of importance" (Piano Concerto). "∧ means 'do not allow this note to weaken,' and often even 'bring out.' (It is mainly up-beats that have been marked thus)" (Quartet, No. 4). Schoenberg's explanations are certainly not equivalent. In the first definition there is no clue to the method by which these notes are to be invested with importance, and, in view of the many methods available, there is no reason to assume that he intended an increase of or fluctuation within the dynamic. The second definition could easily apply to the tenuto mark.

If we construct a definition of the remaining accent mark by combining our previous definitions of the dash and staccato dot, the result is curious indeed: Notes marked ⊤ must be crisp and short, and dull and long. The order of these operations is optional.

Given the following marking

a certain violinist will play a crisp attack on the first quarter note and softer attacks on the others. (Why the difference?) A clarinetist will play three crisp attacks. A tuba player may play three relatively soft but accented attacks. Evidently another cause of our notational dilemma is that each family of instruments has a different idea of the basic attack appropriate to its instruments. (Since strings are trained to connect unmarked notes and winds are trained to separate and to attack them clearly, it may be necessary to notate

for clarinets and

for strings.)

Further investigation reveals that within each family of instruments—indeed within each school of performance within each family—there exist differences of opinion concerning these matters.

The problem is further complicated by the association of articulative marks with mode of expression. But in the past, "expression" usually had longer limits of duration: a section or a movement. When expression was constant within a given tempo, and when tempo itself was used to determine the actual duration of a given note value, it was easier to postulate, if not the proper, at least a consistent concept of duration, dynamic, and mode of attack. Today we are more likely to have diverse expressive components of short duration alternating with great rapidity. Tempo may not have been equated with expressive meaning, and therefore the technical production appropriate to each different element contained within that tempo can in no way be generalized. Unless the symbols of our notation are more rigorously clarified and defined, performers will never be able to realize subtle changes of meaning. If musical expression does exist, it must derive from some complex interrelation of attack, decay, vibrato, tone quality, intonation, dynamic, duration, etc. When each of these terms—as today is the case—is so inconsistently defined that a given specification, while producing a certain audible result in its proper domains, produces, in addition, an audible alteration in other domains, then technical clarity and therefore its attendant expressive clarity is sacrificed.

To summarize, the notation of articulation is very inconsistently associated not only with attack and decay but with duration, dynamic, and the mystery ingredient, expression. But why in this age of 5:3 and twenty (so they say) dynamics should we tolerate such confusion?

Before we can redefine and clarify articulation marks, we must first agree that although pitch cannot be imagined without its modifiers—timbre, loudness, duration, attack and decay, vibrato, etc.—each of these components and their attendant symbologies must, for notational purposes, be regarded as separate and independent. It then follows 1) that the duration of any event will be notated exclusively by a durational symbol, e.g., the staccato dot will no longer be an informal notation for the infinity of notatable durations less than the value of the note to which it applies; 2) that the loudness of any event will be notated exclusively by a loudness symbol, e.g. sforzando will no longer be an informal notation for the infinity of nuances of which

are but a few notatable instances; 3) that articulation and its attendant symbology will be newly defined in terms of attack and decay
characteristics exclusively.[1]

The human voice can probably produce more such articulative
variety than any other instrument; and so, in attempting to characterize attack and decay, I will use modified phonetic symbols that are
more or less equivalent to the effects that can be produced by various
musical instruments. I will not attempt here to establish the articulative limits of each instrument. The lists that follow derive from
general aural experience. While I can state that I am not aware of
ever having heard the tuba produce the sound "ta," I am nevertheless
not prepared to assert that it is incapable of producing this sound. It
is my hope that virtuoso instrumentalists who are interested in this
project will respond by contributing pertinent data in later issues of
this journal.

A general classification of attack possibilities appears on p. 112.

While it is true that the mechanics of most conventional instruments require that certain attack and decay characteristics (especially
when they occur in sequence) be accompanied by changes of dynamic
and duration, these changes—contrary to contemporary practice—can
and must be so slight that they no longer represent aural, and therefore notatable and structurable, phenomena. For instance,

would imply a sharper attack than

but not so sharp as

The notation

correctly performed, would give no auditory sensation of dynamic
change and would be accomplished by shortening the attack time and
ever so slightly increasing the initial dynamic:

[1] Modified applications of these concepts (with more rudimentary symbology)
appear in my Concerto for Wind Quintet (1964) and Piano Concerto (1965).

PHONETIC REPRESENTATION	DESCRIPTION	SUGGESTED SYMBOLOGY	ALTERNATE SYMBOLOGY
1 ta, (ka/ga)	incisive, crisp attacks	•	▾
1a pa, (ba/ma)		ᴗ	•
2 da, (na/la)	weak, delicate attacks	–	–
2a ha, (ja, wa)		h	h
3 (e/o), a	minimized, barely audible or non-existent attacks.	⌒	⌒

Note on pronunciation. "a" as in father, "j" as in yes, "e" as in bet.

From this general classification the following list of modes of attack and decay has been constructed:

> is an operator which when applied to any one of the following symbols intensifies it by increasing its attack rate and dynamic (slightly).

SUGGESTED SYMBOLOGY	ALTERNATE SYMBOLOGY	PHONETIC REPRESENTATION AND DESCRIPTION	VISUAL REPRESENTATION
* ▾	ᴗ▾	tat: incisive, crisp attack with similarly closed decay	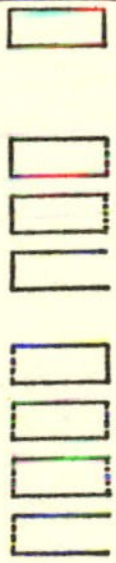
▾ᴗ	∟•	tap	
* •–	∟	tad	
* •	▾	ta: crisp attack with open decay	
ᴗ▾	–┘	pat	
ᴗᴗ	•–	pap	
ᴗ–	•–	pad	
ᴗ	•	pa	
* –▾	–┘	dat	etc.
–ᴗ	–•	dap	
* –∟	–∟	dad	
* –	–	da: weak attack, open decay	
* h▾	h▾	hat	
hᴗ	h•	hap	
* h–	h–	had	
* h	h	ha	
* ⌒▾	⌒▾	at: minimized or inaudible attack, sharp decay	
⌒ᴗ	⌒•	ap	
* ⌒–	⌒–	ad	
* ⌒	⌒	a: minimized or inaudible attack (legato), open decay.	

* As a former clarinetist I think I am correct in asserting that all starred symbols are appropriate to the clarinet.

The old symbols could be eliminated almost entirely:

TT .   TP .   TD .   T .   FT ᵣ   FP .   FD .   P .   ⊓ .   ⊓P .

⊞ .   ⊓ .   FT .   FP .   FD .   H .   ⌢T .   ⌢P .   ⌢D .   ⌢ .

In order that the number of symbols might be reduced, I would recommend that all unmarked notes be regarded as members of the ta-ka family.

would then be taken to mean

I would further recommend that the markings be notated in the same manner for all instruments, thus ending such famous historical confusions as the meaning of

The newly defined articulation marks would solve such fundamental questions as how to specify two notes of the same medium dynamic when the first is incisively attacked and the second is legato. In traditional notation there is no way to guarantee this result. We would solve the dynamic problem by writing *mp sempre* but the desired attack could not be indicated. A dot

(e.g., ♫)

might yield the proper result but it could not be applied without contradicting the fundamental durational meaning. We would probably write

♫
mp sempre

—and pray. In new notation

♫
mp

would suffice—though not without prayer.

Here is a short excerpt in new notation:

Clarinet or Violin:

(Remember that the staccato dot is assumed for unmarked notes.)

Note in m. 1 that the pitches need not be connected by slurs since their decay characteristics imply maximal connection. If separation were desired the appropriate rests would be inserted:

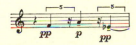

Before passing judgment on this system the reader is asked to attempt an exact renotation of the excerpt using conventional symbols.

1966

FOR THE FLUTE: A LIST OF DOUBLE-STOPS, TRIPLE-STOPS, QUADRUPLE-STOPS, AND SHAKES

JOHN C. HEISS

WHILE multiple-stops on the flute are not so numerous or flexible as on stringed instruments, they nonetheless represent a legitimate, and, to my knowledge, little-used extension of what the flute is presumed to be able to do. Most of them are available only as sounds of very short duration, which are not generally capable of being sustained in spite of the fact that they are quite easy to produce. In the case of the double-stops, for instance, the player must "aim" between the two given tones in order to make both sound: attempts to sustain both result in the predominance of one or the other.

Some further instructions are as follows. For the triple- and quadruple-stops, the player should try to "spread" his tone, making it cover a broad spectrum in order to include each of the pitches involved. (This is done by using a wider aperture in the hole between the lips, so as to direct the air column both "high" and "low" at the same time.) In playing the sounds of short duration, the best result is obtained with a short, articulate, and carefully directed burst of air. The "spread" tone is best for those sounds which can be sustained.

My impulse to search for these sonorities came from two sources. A flutist-colleague[1] introduced me to the double-stop given as number 1 on my list. Also, a remarkable and complex "blaring" sound known to bassoonists, and used by George Perle in the first of his Three Inventions for Solo Bassoon,[2] suggested the possible existence of a wide variety of compositionally useful sounds available from other woodwinds, and not hitherto employed.

Acoustically, these sonorities probably result from overtone relationships and/or fingerings which provide two or more possible tube-lengths for use in the production of tone. Many of the double-stops, for example, are produced by opening one or both of the two trill holes nearest the head joint in conjunction with closing a succession of the larger holes along the main body of the instrument. This enables the player to use either a short tube-length or a somewhat longer one, or, if he so desires, to use both simul-

taneously. (The fingerings for the third octave of the flute are based on this principle. Here, tube-lengths which reinforce one another are used to produce the tone which is their lowest common partial.)

---

[1] David Shostac, first-chair flutist with the New Orleans Philharmonic.

[2] The sound was suggested to Mr. Perle by the bassoonist William Scribner, of New York City. Mr. Perle advises that the *Inventions* are not yet published, and that his present intention is either to add more sounds of this type, or to remove the sound altogether and use a group of such sounds in a later context.

	Left Hand	Right Hand
1 * – 1a – 1b – 1c – 1d	Th, 2, 3, 4 (1–1b) / Th, 2, 3, 4 (1c–1d)	2, 3(tr), 4(tr) / 2, 3(tr), 4(tr), 5(D)
2 – 2a – 2b – 3 – 3a	Th, 3, 4 / Th, 2, 3, 4	2, 3(tr), 4(E) / 3(tr), 4 [or 3, 4(tr)]
4 – 4a – 5 – 6 – 6a	Th, 2, 3, 4 / Th, 3, 4 / Th, 3, 4	2, 3(tr, nearest to 2) / — / 2
7 – 8 – 9 – 9a	Th, 3, 4 / Th, 3, 4, 5 / Th, 3 / Th, 3	2, 3 / 2, 3, 4, 5(E♭) / 5(E♭) / 2, 3(open-hole) and 5(E♭)
10 – 11 – 12 – 12a – 12b	Th, 2, 3 / Th(B♭), 2, 4 / Th, 3, 4	2, 3, 4(tr) / 2(tr), 3, 4 / 2, 3, 4(slightly open), 5(E♭)
13 – 14	Th(B♭), 2 / Th, 2, 4	2(tr), 3(tr) / 2, 3(tr), 4(E), 5(D)

* Try this:

Note: 9a and 12-12a-12b cannot be attained on a closed-hole flute.

My notations are conventional. *Th, 2, 3, 4,* and *5* refer to fingers. Parentheses surround instructions as to the particular key to be depressed by a given finger. *Tr* stands for "trill-key." Where there are no parentheses the given fingers depress those keys with which they are normally associated. Black notes indicate short duration; white notes indicate combinations which can be sustained.

Four of the shakes (numbers 4-7) are obtainable through other, more normal, fingers than those given here. My fingerings, however, produce unique effects, which differ considerably from what one would customarily expect in writing the particular intervals. In numbers 8-13 three or more tones are involved in each of the resultant sonorities. The sizes of the noteheads refer to the relative intensities of the tones (larger noteheads to louder tones, smaller noteheads to softer ones). When no other instructions are given, arrows indicate the key which is to be trilled.

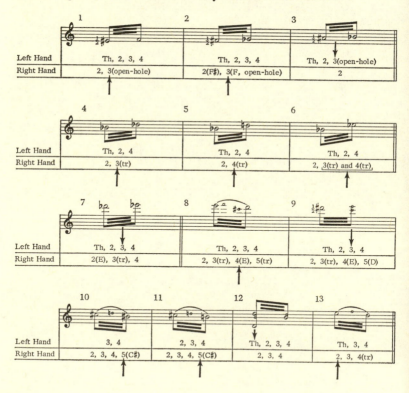

A DESCRIPTIVE LANGUAGE
FOR THE ANALYSIS OF
ELECTRONIC MUSIC

BRIAN FENNELLY

WITH THE absence of available musical scores, the aural experience is the single point of departure for the analysis of electronic music. In approaching any music by this method the analyst must confront the actual sound; the ear is his only guide. Discussion can stem only from concentrated listening and careful evaluation of the perceived phenomena. The results of such an approach may reveal discrepancies between the aural analysis and one done only from a score, pointing perhaps to inadequacy in auralizing the printed note or to a particular fallibility of the ear. Deviations may also arise between analytical results and a composer's intentions, if known. In this light aural analysis can be a test for the effectiveness of realization of the composer's aims. At the same time it tests the analyst's own acuity and will easily reveal that a particular piece may have several facets to which any individual may respond.

The literature of electronic music has recently been the subject of two kinds of aurally-oriented investigations at the Yale University studio. The more general test gleaned broad observations on formal characteristics and properties of texture from a group of student composers and performers in the Yale School of Music. Given two short pieces (by Babbitt and Boulez), with the number of hearings and the time allowed for decisions limited, the majority of the group coped well with the analytic tasks. As might be expected, the work of those with compositional experience exhibited more sophistication. Textural descriptions relied heavily on analogies with familiar sounds, instrumental and otherwise. The medium itself did not serve as an appreciable obstacle to those who approached the project without preconceptions.

The other project required more detailed analytic work from members of a class of student theorists and composers, all of whom were gaining insight into basic studio techniques. Several weeks were allowed for the preparation of individual papers analyzing a short work (Franco Evangelisti's *Incontri di fascie sonore*) for subsequent seminar discussion.

Severe problems arose while attempting to isolate and characterize certain elements without lengthy and often labored descriptions. The lack of a system by which the "orchestration" of any passage might be concisely defined was a barrier to group communication, thwarting formulation and discussion at the desired level of detail. Hence the motivation for the present project: to provide a systematic, straight-forward means for the concise identification and characterization of sounds encountered in the tape literature.

The aural experience was designated as the point of orientation for this system; it was from here that analysis was to proceed. The specific nature of the derivation of a given sound would not be an aspect of the language, as this would require prior knowledge as to source and manipulation. Presumably such information would lie outside of the analyst's grasp. The lack of such data would not alter the relevance or potency of his tools, which however do depend in part on a basic familiarity with the indigenous electronic sources and modes of transformation. The effects of various ways of filtering, reverberation, etc. upon several sources, as well as examples of different modes of attack and decay, must be made available to the novice for intensive study. Such a compilation is a kind of introduction to the "orchestral instruments" and their capabilities. A textural analysis of orchestration, conventional or electronic, can proceed only after such groundwork has been accomplished.

The envisioned system must seek several kinds of balance. In the incorporation of technical terms, the disparity in knowledge of studio processes between the intended analyst and the experienced composer must be considered. A second balance must be found in the inclusion of terms that rely on analogy or onomatopoeia. While convenient in con-ceptualizing sounds, such terms can be bulky and awkward in context. A third consideration is necessary in regard to the scope and degree of specificity of the system elements. While an extensive, detailed symbology lends an air of precision, it can be inflexible and become an undesirable obstacle to learning the language. The precision of the ear itself and its powers of differentiation will dictate the limits of the system. Ideally, the symbols will associate readily with the matter described and will have additional qualities of simplicity and convenience of handling. Rather than a complex body of terms, a flexible core capable of extension and development for the particular instance is desirable.

The very nature of the electronic medium requires the terminology to permit overlapping means of description to cover, for example, the continuum formed by the combination of pitched components proceeding from the exactly tuned chord, through the area of non-harmonic mix-tures, to the dense nature of frequency relations of the components of a noise band-width. Between the outer limits and the mixtures, the borders are indistinct, especially in the context of a composition. Provisions must be made so that the descriptive language itself is capable of such smooth transitions, so that there are areas which can be defined in terms of either pole and at the same time made to relate to the other.

The possible kinds of descriptive systems within the limitations imposed above are few. The precision of a completely technical language is impossible because the product is heard only in its finished form; the stages of realization are unknown. On the other hand, such an abstract language would not be apt to convey the aural image as readily as desired. The antithesis of this system type would be a synthetic vocabulary whose words contain by phonic analogy the attack and timbral characteristics of the musical sounds they represent. While the aural association here would be direct, such an approach is cumbersome and would be difficult to employ with a proper measure of consistency. Its comical implications are obvious. There are, however, certain noise-related sounds whose character can be described onomatopoeically in a manner more efficient than any other system. The use of the vocabulary of conventional instrumental sounds and sounds of nature as referential sonorities where analogy to electronic sound can be made comprises another point of departure. A workable solution must find some comfortable middle ground that can include the most useful features of each. In combining terms derived from such unrelated avenues of approach each must be allowed to participate in a complementary manner to function most effectively.

In evolving a body of terms there are certain initial assumptions and definitions to be made. Since the analytic language is divorced from the derivational process, terminology common to both must be regarded as purely descriptive in the former. Such terms cannot be construed to specify process, even though they may actually apply, but will only represent events whose features are typical of the results of the given processes. This applies to both source and transformation terms. In using terms arising from comparisons with environmental sounds, an additional stipulation is necessary. Given an event timbrally related to the piano, the language will make this association regardless of its relevancy to sound derivation; it will also exist apart from and transcend any aesthetic questions involving the propriety of particular source materials.

The admission of both electronic signals (of necessity) and natural analogs (for convenience) to the fund of "sound images" points to a further need: consistency of notation. Whereas the designation of a sound as "piano-like" infers certain properties of attack and decay, the designation "filtered sawtooth" contains no such inferences, as the latter is a steady state phenomenon in its unmodified form. A notation must be devised to accomodate both, so that not only the timbre but the envelope and other features of a sound may be represented in a brief standardized format. The inevitable basis of the language is a formula whose terms separately represent the components of a sound in rank of their perceptual importance: first timbre, with means of describing spectrum adjustments, then the envelope controls of attack type and dynamic curve. A third term would be useful for designating any further defining characteristics, as beating, amplitude oscillations of certain spectrum components, or use of reverberation. These last features collectively will be given the generous title "Enhancement." With symbols as follows—timbre X_S of timbre type X and spectrum S, envelope Y_C of attack Y and continuation C, and enhancement E—the general formula for the description of any sound is $X_S Y_C E$. This formula will permit description not only of the single sound but can apply also to linear "voices" or groups of elements of identical timbre and attack. Additionally, the individual terms may be extracted for discussions of a more general nature, e.g., a particular timbral type without regard to envelope or without regard to particular spectral adjustments. Isolation of a particular attack type or spectrum control regardless of timbre are other possibilities. Use of lower-case symbols, defined in the course of the following discussion, for secondary characteristics can eventually expand the formula to $X_{Sr}{}^t Y_{Cd}{}^i E$.*

Implementation now rests upon adequate subdivision and categorization of the areas defined by each of the formula symbols. Decisions concerning the nature and extent of the subdivisions must be primarily based on practicality, as each of these areas possesses characteristics of a continuum.

Timbre X_S

Timbral composition depends on spectral frequency characteristics, where a broad area exists between what is perceived as definitely pitched and definitely non-pitched (noise). In this transitional zone the ear perceives pitch area characteristics. In the case of a group of simple tones forming a "mistuned chord," it tries to rationalize and adjust the tuning. While the latter is clearly a pitched event, other events may be borderline. The language will indicate only two general areas: pitch-related sound, with a fundamental or a particular predominant tone, and noise-related sound. These concepts are quite broad in nature. The

---

* AUTHOR'S NOTE. Where both subscripts and superscripts occur for any X, Y, or E, the author prefers a style in which the upper index (or indices) is placed directly above the lower index. Due to production difficulties in type composition, this was impossible. It is therefore left to the reader to accomplish the necessary transposition to arrive at the original notation.

exact point of division between the two areas in any given context must be decided upon by the individual auditor for his own reference. Since the language is meant to reflect a personal evaluation, this point is critical as an appraisal of how each individual's perception operates.

The previously discussed "sound images"—those sounds most easily auralized from a given description—are of two kinds: the basic electronic signals and the environmentally related sounds. While the generated signals are limited in number, there is little restriction on possible natural analogs. A listing of symbols for the latter is therefore impractical. In devising class groupings for timbral types, these are placed under general headings, while the perceptually significant distinctions between the electronic signals serve as bases for their separation into different classes. See Table I, timbre type X. I and II are the pitch-related and noise-related divisions, respectively. Classes 1, 2, and 5 cover the

TABLE I: Timbre X$_S$

Timbre type X:

I
1. sine wave
2. square or sawtooth wave
3. combinations*
4. "natural" (environmental analog)

II
5. white noise
6. combinations*
7. "natural" (environmental analog)

I.—pitched, with fundamental or predominant tone

II.—noise-related

* combinations of several sources perceived as a single unit

Spectrum subscript S:

‡ G.   full, or nearly full spectrum
† H.   high components only
≠ MH. midrange and high components
⊦ M.   midrange only
≰ LM. midrange and lows
⊥ L.   low components only
‡ LH. lows and highs only, midrange out
    F*. fluctuating

* Special cases of F:

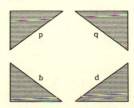

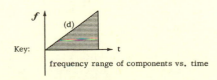

Key:

frequency range of components vs. time

Superscript t indicating timbre-class interrelation:

for X classes: 1, 2, 5:   class 4 or 7 abbreviations if related to natural timbral
types (the timbre first having been defined as 1, 2, or 5)

                 3, 6:   class 4 or 7 abbreviations and class numbers 1, 2, 5 to
identify timbral qualities

                 4, 7:   class numbers 1, 2, 5 if related, or other class 4 and 7
abbreviations

Second subscript r denoting general registral placement:

0 very low
1 low
2 medium low
3 midrange
4 medium high
5 high
6 very high

Approximate boundaries:

electronic timbres; square and sawtooth waveforms are grouped together, since they are usually impossible to distinguish in the context of a piece. Classes 4 and 7 encompass the wide gamut of natural analogs. Thus while each of the first-mentioned classes defines a timbral type, classes 4 and 7 are non-homogeneous. Notation of natural analogs will require nominal abbreviations for identification, as V = vocal, Pno = Piano, BD = bass drum, etc. A key is obviously necessary for any abbreviations used.

Two further classes, 3 and 6, are provided for the residual timbres which do not have the limited characteristics of the basic electronic signals and for which no environmental analog can be envisioned. The designation "combination" implies the probability that such sounds are the result of more than one source signal, yet combined so that the result is perceived as a single unit. Formations where individual pitched elements can be isolated, such as chords, are the most straightforward examples of class 3. Chord formations can be defined either as class 3 members or as "chords composed of tones X_S," X_S indicating the timbral nature of the individual tones. The latter method specifically indicates the chordal nature, whereas the former indicates only membership in the class of pitched combinations. Expectedly, the dividing line between classes 3 and 6 is inexact; e.g., the sine-tone mixtures encountered in the first Cologne Studio efforts are often borderline as to their designation here, depending on the number and frequency relation of their components. As these two classes do not define timbral qualities, this is accomplished with superscripts to be discussed later.

The "fine tuning" adjustment for timbre description is the spectrum subscript S. While the spectrum range symbols are defined as results of the subtractive process of filtering a complex spectrum, these same symbols apply also to spectra resulting from sine-tone superimposition. Here the symbols must be interpreted as defining a spectrum which is the result of the additive process of selecting and combining certain frequencies in a chosen intensity relation. Symbol G would imply the addition of many partials, symbol L the pure or nearly pure sine wave. Symbols H, MH, and M have little meaning in this context except to indicate portions of a synthesized harmonic series whose fundamental is missing. These three symbols are much more explicit in regard to timbre classes 2 or 5, where spectrum characteristics resulting from filtering are predictable. The second set of symbols contained in the far left column is presented because their graphic nature may be more appealing for handwritten work.

Not only does the spectrum subscript pinpoint timbre more exactly, it allows the timbre classes of environmental analogs to encompass more of the sound phenomena of the electronic medium. The timbre type designation is considered to be equivalent to the unmodified source; an analysis of the possibilities of spectral modification of any natural sound will appreciably increase the number of environmental relations that can be made. It is possible, for example, to auralize the timbral nature of a gong with all but the lowest frequencies removed, or a modified bassoon timbre. Definitely the most useful area will be in finding analogs for noise-related sounds.

The final spectrum symbol F defines a spectrum which is not stable. The simple cases of such a characteristic are those in which the spectrum begins at a certain band-width and widens or narrows, up or down. For convenience, each of the letter symbols used to designate these features is by its particular geometry related to the spectrum with which it is identified. Combinations of these symbols can be employed to define spectra which can be broken down into simple components, e.g., db, symbols in succession, to indicate spectrum change from lows only upwards and back again; or $_p$d, symbols simultaneously, indicating introduction of highs as the lows are filtered out. A more precise description may be apt in some circumstances, using subclasses of F in conjunction with the other spectrum subscripts: e.g., $_q$dG where G indicates that the point of arrival is the full spectrum; or even more precise, M_qdG additionally indicating the initial state of the spectrum to be midrange only. The combination LMp indicates upward filtering operating on spectrum LM until it is obliterated; LMpM indicates that such filtering is dampened to leave midrange elements untouched. The degree to which such detail is required will depend on the analyst's purpose; a composer using the language for an informal score may wish to be specific here. In the analyst's case, it is obvious that only where such detail can be apprehended aurally is this description permitted at all. Where there is evidence of changing spectrum, impossible to analyze, the general symbol F must suffice.

Additional adjuncts to timbre type have been devised to further clarify the timbral description. The superscript t to X varies in importance according to the timbre class with which it is used. For classes 3 and 6 it supplies timbral information lacking in the timbre type designation. For the remaining classes it is of use only when some timbre-type interrelation obtains. With classes 1, 2, and 5, and most natural analogs, it provides an additional refinement by relating a secondary timbral image to a defined timbre type, indicating an intersection of the two. Some common examples might be: a class 2 waveform filtered almost to the point of a sine wave, $2_L{}^1$; the bassoon-like $2_{LM}{}^{bsn}$ or tuba-like $2_L{}^{tba}$; a bell-like sound with sine-tone structure, $bell^1$. In the case of vocally related sound, the superscript is actually timbre defining, since various timbres are possible with the voice. Hence V^5 can be used to denote the vocal "sh." It is also possible to notate vowel sounds. This use of the superscript with such a flexible instrument as the voice involves stipulation as to which of the possible sound types is desired. A similar procedure may obtain with other instruments concerning the mode of sound production, e.g., VC^{pizz} for pizzicato cello, Pno^{mute} for keyboard sound with muted strings.

A second subindex r to X accommodates a scheme to locate sounds within the frequency continuum. The nature of the subdivision arises from practicality, providing a convenient number of registral areas, each of sufficiently broad range. The boundaries indicated are only approximate, dividing the continuum into equal parts except for the two extremes. This subscript is most useful in fixing the pitch-area location of noise-related sound, or in defining the ambitus of an instrumental line. Symbols can be joined to indicate larger areas.

Envelope Y_C

The two basic components Y and subscript C define the incipient transient state and the subsequent nature of the dynamic curve respectively. With Y_C coupled to X_S, timbral description can be fitted with appropriate envelope characteristics that define both a particular attack type (which in the case of conventional instruments is critical to identification) and the nature of continuation of the sound. The latter depends on whether or not the "instrument" is capable of sustaining its sounds; it is made either to decay at a given rate or to adjust or maintain its dynamic continuation at will. While the variations possible in the latter case are manifold, the nature of simple decay makes it desirable to make measurement of the length of the sound possible as an index of still another instrument-defining characteristic. In other instances measurement of time between attacks can indicate the pacing of a line. Implementation of such will be made through addition to the Y_C term.

Table II sets forth the designation system for the envelope components. Since envelope characteristics function in time, the components are defined in terms of change or rate of change of amplitude with respect to

TABLE II: Envelope Y_C

Attack Y:

A   very slow growth
B   slow growth
C   moderate growth
D   rapid growth
O   attack imperceptible

Continuation subscript C:

a   steady state
b   increasing intensity (crescendo)
c   decreasing intensity (diminuendo)
d   not classifiable due to context
f   fluctuating intensity (possibly defined in terms of a, b, & c)

Superscript i to denote intensity relation of Y to C:

l   loud
m   medium
s   soft
o   attack characteristics appear to be without transients

Second subscript d indicating general area of component duration or signal pacing: (Symbols define a "duration register" or speed range of specified ambitus.)

Symbols:	very short	short		moderate		long		very long
	S (less than ⅛″)	S		M		L		L (8″ or more)
		s	s	ms	ml	l	l	
Duration in seconds:	⅛	¼	½	1	2	4	8	

Boundary point
Equivalents
at ♩ = 60:

the time element. The attack types under Y are distinguished by different rates of growth of the incipient elements of signals. This is in proportion to the perceived degree of firmness of the attack. The 0 class accommodates the case of the sound which emerges from silence with its beginning undetectable. The term "attack transients" has been avoided deliberately in this discussion since the electronic medium is capable of projecting a signal without transient frequency or amplitude characteristics. Any transient elements present under such conditions are transients of response to the recorded signal in the playback system, the acoustic environment, and the ear. Such a signal falls within the attack groups specified as one of rapid growth—a case in which the growth is instantaneous from zero to full amplitude. The lack of transients does not necessarily divest such a sound of elegance, although its qualities are often quite distinctive. Other signals lacking noise transients characteristic of conventional instruments can similarly be accommodated by the particular method of attack definition here employed.

The basic continuation types under subscript C are most elementary: steady state, crescendo, and diminuendo. In contexts where tone continuation cannot be apprehended because of masking by other elements or the rapidity of a passage, symbol d denotes this problem. The final category f encompasses those dynamic curves other than the most simple ones enumerated. A relation between this letter designation and the F of fluctuating spectrum can be noted. Spectrum changes can be accompanied by changes in intensity, whether actual or only apparent; the symbological relation of the two not only portrays the analogy of common processes of fluctuation but also connotes the possibility of the perceiver's association of spectrum adjustment with intensity change, however slight. (Such "apparent" intensity change is not likely to be significant in a context where the attention is drawn primarily to the spectrum activity.) The compound dynamic curves of f proceed from the common espressivo ($<\ >$) which is notated as the combination bc, to those containing numerous changes, possibly at speeds too rapid to allow breakdown into simple components. It is obvious that the value of such an analysis in terms of basic dynamic changes will differ according to the situation and the nature of the investigation. The ease with which such analysis can be done is in proportion to the perceptual significance of the ordering of the components. Rapidly fluctuating dynamic curves tend toward similarity; their common characteristic of fluctuation is more noticeable than the difference between the specific orders of dynamic changes. Hence dynamic component analysis is apt to have value only where the individual changes are markedly apparent and is prescribed primarily for clarification of the least involved situations, as bc, bac, etc., and slowly paced unfoldings where the nature of the curve is evident and relevant to the gesture of the sound.

Further categories of descriptive data that can be appended to the present Y_C are of two kinds, both pertinent to elucidation of the Y_C term itself. The first describes the intensity relation of the attack to the immediately following part of the signal, allowing more precision in formulation of attack properties. This takes the form of superscript i, of which there are four types as listed in Table II. The final symbol will convey the peculiar qualities of the situation where there is an apparent absence of attack transients. The remaining symbols represent degree of intensity relation on a very broad basis of division.

The second category comprises a method of correlating the envelope with a scheme of durational measurement. This is the second subscript to Y, designated d. Here again, the particular instance will dictate the degree of accuracy required. The system permits two kinds of use: durational measurement of single sounds, and measurement of distance between attack points in an instrumental line. The first denotes time displaced by a sound, the second generates a concept of the rate of flow or pacing of signals. The meaning will be evident from the nature of the matter undergoing description, as the symbolic characterization of a timbrally continuous line must be identified as such to differentiate it from the single sound. The two interpretations can be seen in the following: "an instrumental line composed of elements $X_S Y_{Cd}$" (d = duration of each individual element) and "an instrumental line $X_S Y_{Cd}$" (d = average distance between attacks within the line, $X_S Y_C$ defines the instrumental character).

The method of duration measurement permits three degrees of accuracy. Highly generalized categorization is achieved by use of the S S M L L divisions shown in Table II. Subdivision of the S M L groups as accomplished by the lower-case symbols provides finer definition of the most frequently encountered areas. In contrast to these rather informal, pre-established partitions of the time continuum, the third type of notation permits a precision whose limitations are prescribed only by the auditor's skill. In place of a symbol denoting a duration area the measured numerical value in seconds or fractions of a second is employed for the d subscript. This type of measurement is most appropriate in conjunction with indication of rates of speed. The composer using this language in preparing a score will prefer such numerical measurement as the most accurate record of his work.

The duration subscript is of still further use in isolating envelope characteristics. In the case of the compound dynamic curve defined by a combination of the continuation subscripts a, b, and c, the resulting composite term gives no indication of the relative weights of the constituent elements with regard to that portion of the total time each element displaces. The desire to include such information may arise in certain cases, e.g., that of a long sound containing both rapid and slowly unfolding changes in envelope. While seldom critical to the analyst, such data is of interest to the composer and may be recorded by a succession of C and d subscripts in which each d value associates with the preceeding C symbol: $Y_{C_1 d_1 C_2 d_2 \cdots C_n d_n}$.

Enhancement E

The gathering of all further characteristics of a sound under the heading "Enhancement" is a convenience rather than an appraisal of their contribution to the elegance of a particular event; neither does it indicate the presence of any common aspect binding these properties together into a group. There are, however, subgroups as can be seen in Table III, to be discussed in turn.

The initial symbol 0 denotes the lack of any sonorous qualities beyond those covered by the X and Y terms of the formula. In the case of the electronic signal this can give evidence of a certain baldness in the quality of the sound. Since natural analogs are by nature richer in quality, this symbol associated with them does not of necessity have such a connotation.

The four E elements related to the use of reverberation deal with the "live" aspects of a sound. The symbol nr distinctly specifies a lack of reverberation in contrast to the more inclusive symbol 0. The next two terms deal with the degree of enlivenment, while the final R_o denotes the presence of the echo alone, apparently uncoupled from the input signal. Such a sound has a hollow quality and usually lacks incisiveness in the attack.

The two types of vibrato listed are to be distinguished by the degree to which they do or do not resemble what would be a normal vibrato on a conventional instrument of appropriate register and tone color

TABLE III: Enhancement E

0	none		
nr	no reverberation	v	"natural" vibrato
r	some noticeable reverberation	V	"abnormal" vibrato
R	high reverberation		
R_o	reverberation only	b	beating
g	glissando during decay (↑↓)	I	iteration
G	glissando connecting pitch levels (↑↓)	FB	feedback
VS	variable speed	L	use of loops
AM	amplitude modulation other than vibrato		
FM	frequency modulation other than vibrato		

approximate to the sound under observation. It is, in effect, a measure of the success of a simulated vibrato in persuading the auditor of its authenticity. Such a decision must not be regarded as purely qualitative, as the measure is essentially quantitative—the "unnatural" vibrato is apt to be unusually wide or rigidly periodic.

Confusion with vibrato can sometimes occur in detecting the presence of a beating frequency, denoted by the symbol b. Usually the singularity of the beating phenomenon is conspicuous, so that instances of similarity between the two are few. To pinpoint the identity of these instances for purposes of auralization a composite term suggests itself: the beating symbol with the appropriate vibrato symbol as a superscript.

Distinction is made between a glissando during the continuation of a single sound or totality of sounds (g) and the use of glissando in sliding from one pitch level to another, i.e., portamento (G). The latter is essentially an aspect of melodic inflection. Optional arrows indicate the direction of the change in frequency. The VS term indicates a glissando of a less conventional nature that can be regarded as a product of varying the tape speed. The character of this situation is rather unusual because of the transparency of its technical means. Use of the VS term thus alludes to a certain obviousness of technique, which is often equated with a lack of refinement of gesture. However, the latter is clearly an aesthetic issue which must remain outside the concerns of this descriptive system.

Use of the symbols for amplitude modulation and frequency modulation is presumed to exclude definition of situations where these techniques are involved in the production of vibrato. When it is necessary to indicate mode of vibrato production they can become superscripts to the appropriate vibrato term. Otherwise, AM and FM are reserved for special instances, e.g., individual amplitude variation of the internal components of a mixture. This is to be distinguished from amplitude change in the envelope Y_C, which pertains to the large span dynamic curve of the composite sound. Similarly, wavering of pitch or warbling lie within the domain of the FM symbol, as these are outside the bounds of the concept of vibrato. FM is not to be confused with adjustments to the timbral spectrum.

The final group of E terms deals with three types of signal repetition encountered primarily in the composition of timbral and linear musical texture. The symbol I denotes the presence of an iterated quantity within the body of a larger unit that is perceived as a single sound. It is essential that such iteration contribute to the sonorous quality of the larger unit rather than exist as an independent entity, otherwise it would have to be defined as a series of separate signals.

The presence of acoustic feedback FB is easily detected. While it involves echoing of a signal or series of signals, its significance is also primarily textural, here with respect to the linear density of the music. In the statement X_SY_CFB, X_SY_C defines the initial signal and FB denotes the presence of any number of after-images.

While loop technique can be the source of ostinato, it is also of use in assembling a montage of sounds whose components lose individuality and cannot be distinguished, much like a crowd noise. Hence L indicates the quality of inner confusion that exists in such a composite sound. When concerned with an ostinato, L refers to the repetition of the sound or sequence of sounds defined by the preceding terms of the formula.

Further aspects that would fall under the Enhancement term may be occasionally encountered, such as deliberate distortion of the recorded signal employed as a timbral adjunct. Appropriate symbols readily suggest themselves for such procedures. The arrows associated with the glissando terms might also be applied in a horizontal direction to indicate reversal of such processes as reverberation or feedback. In the vertical direction, they can denote an increasing (upward) or decreasing rate of vibrato or beating.

Provisions have been made for indicating the nature of practically every possible aspect of an event with the exception of its dynamic level, for which the conventional symbols suffice. It is unnecessary to append these to the present formula, which is quite detailed in its most complete stage, unless specification of critical intensity values of a changing dynamic curve is desired. Requirements for the full formula may be infrequent, but such detail is always possible; the appropriate subscripts or superscripts can be selected to deal with particular needs.

The inclusion of any type of onomatopoeic description into this language has not been discussed. As noted earlier, some sounds may lend themselves more readily to this approach than to any other including the present analytic system. The identity of a complex entity that is the phonic representation of a total sound would be placed in jeopardy were it to be subject to dismemberment for accommodation into the X_SY_C formula. The most practical solution allows such terms to maintain their integral nature and permits their existence as adjuncts to the system, outside of the X_SY_C symbology. Still, for maximum consistency and ease of inspection and correlation of final analytic results, this technique should be invoked only in those complex situations to which onomatopoeia is particularly adaptable and in which X_SY_C component analysis would be unusually difficult to perform and auralize.

Within the language onomatopoeia can function in a quite flexible manner by the admission of certain short words, i.e., Buzz, Hiss, etc., to the categories of natural analogs. As the environmental analog possesses by nature a suggestion of the total sound rather than only its timbral composition, such words can be displayed quite comfortably within the broader condition of X class signification that applies here. Their usefulness is to be found particularly in making timbral cross-relations by means of superscript t.

A further use of phonic analogy can be accomplished when vowel formant characteristics are detected in a spectrum; here the prescribed spectrum symbology can be replaced by the properly related vowel sound. The presence of such non-linear characteristics in spectrum component intensity can be indicated more generally by underlining the range in which the peak occurs, as $S = LMH$ in the case of a full spectrum with emphasized highs. By the same token a full spectrum whose midrange intensity has been partially reduced might be notated $L\overline{M}H$, the upper dash denoting a decrease in emphasis. These modifications to the symbology are essentially extensions of the basic design to increase the specificity of its terminology.

A need to modify the basic X and Y classes should not arise, although these groups in the hands of the composer might yield to specification of the actual sources and attack processes involved. The results of the use of such studio devices as the electronic switch and ring modulator submit themselves to description by the presented terminology without invoking procedural terms. Here again, the composer may prefer inclusion of such data. The electronic switch used as a source of impulses is not mentioned in the electronic timbral classes, as each of the impulses consists of a white noise band, X class 5. As a group these impulses either define a frequency belonging to class 2 or exist as an iterative quantity, depending on the speed of the pulse train.

Adaptations of the given symbology can be envisioned to accommodate a variety of complex situations. Given a particular sequence of signals of X_SY_C subjected first to ostinato treatment (L) and then to further dynamic curve and enhancement operations, brackets and parentheses can be utilized to indicate the different levels to which such operations pertain: (X_SY_CL) $Y'_{C'}E'$. Y' specifies the initial attack of the whole; it might be identical with the Y within the quantity. If a spectrum change is in evidence at the higher level, this would be shown as a subscript to the quantity in parentheses, which is the X upon which this second group of operations acts. An example of such a totality is $(2_{LM}D_CL)_{db}O_{bc}R$. The notation of this event points up the succinct quality of the language. Preparation of a concise verbal description capable of quick evaluation and easy comparison with similar descriptions of other events would be a difficult task. Use of and familiarity with the symbolic language promotes the desired ease of recognition and correlation. While convenient for both analyst and composer, the latter may favor a more precise record of certain aspects of his operations. Such data as actual source material, frequency, filter and reverberation settings, db levels, etc., can be specified concurrently with the symbolic notation. Adaptation to align the language with useful features of conventional musical notation is also possible.

The value of this language as a method of sonic representation has been demonstrated. As an analytic tool it is capable of clearly indicating relations between events as well as suggesting relations that might not be readily noticed under other systems. Any laxity in notation that might lead to misrepresentation of events and erroneous evaluations must be avoided. In the course of analysis, relations suggested by the notation require re-inspection of the phenomena involved to ascertain, first, the correctness of the interpretation of the quantities and their symbolic reductions, and, second, the degree and relevance of their relation.

An example of this language applied to an electronic work available on disc recording will best serve to illustrate the technique. The short *Fragment* of Bülent Arel (on Son-Nova 3) is an ideal vehicle, as it encompasses a variety of sounds in a straightforward presentation. The

example (p. 132) is the opening segment of a complete analysis made for didactic purposes, arrived at solely by aural evaluation of the commercially recorded version. The informal graphic scheme is intended merely as a guide to reading and does not indicate attack points or durations. Note how the X subscript r becomes valuable when dealing with filtered noise, where the S symbols can indicate filtering only loosely because of the range of the spectrum involved.

Conspicuous features that occur later in the *Fragment* are the ostinato frog-like sounds and rumbles. The final ostinato occurrence, $64''-69''$, is like cricket chirping: $(3_{L3}{}^{crkts}C_a{}^oL)Y_c$. The low rumble that begins at $70''$ and persists almost to the end undergoes spectrum change which can be defined registrally by use of the r symbols: $5_{2q12dl-3}{}^{rumble}0_a AM_{trem}$. The AM symbol indicates the tremulous quality of the sound.

1967

PROGRAMMED SIGNALS
TO PERFORMERS:
A NEW COMPOSITIONAL RESOURCE

EMMANUEL GHENT

RHYTHM HAS been a most unyielding problem in recent music, as viewed from the difficulties it presents in notation, performance, and perception, not to mention the very process of composition itself. It is the purpose of this paper to describe a method for transmitting programmed signals to performers both as an approach to simplifying certain problems of notation and performance, and as a resource designed to extend rhythmic horizons for the composer. By way of a postlude I will present a closely related system of electronic music synthesis.

Before entering into the details of the present approach, it is germane to review the role of pulse in the history of Western music. The passage of the Middle Ages witnessed the end of an era of great rhythmic flexibility. Musicians of the day must have been remarkably skilled in the by now almost lost art of proportional tempo discrimination.[1] The new epoch of the barline did provide for several centuries an immensely useful scaffolding for musical composition and performance, but at the same time imposed the tyranny of the steady beat from which composers have been delivering themselves ever since. The unshackling devices in earlier periods include the use of rubato, recitative, the fermata, displaced accents, and syncopation. In the twentieth century the pace accelerated with the introduction of a succession of rhythmic innovations eroding more and more the role of the steady pulse, often by supplying new dimensions of rhythmic structure. By way of a few illustrations, one need only recall the additive rhythms, or what might be called the aperiodic pulse, of Stravinsky and Bartók, the polytempo writing of Ives, the rhythmic ostinati of Varèse, and more recently the rhythmic sculptures of Shapey, Carter's rhythmic modulation, the architectonic pulselessness of Webern, the serialization of rhythmic relationships, the flux of shifting densities whose purpose is the avoidance of any sense of pulse, and

[1] Cf. Charles Wuorinen, "Notes on the Performance of Contemporary Music," PERSPECTIVES OF NEW MUSIC, Vol. 3, No. 1, pp. 10–22.

finally aleatoric relationships. Along with these developments came changes in notation. The barline lost its meaning and was abandoned, sometimes in favor of proportional or analog notation. In much contemporary writing, regardless of the theoretical underpinnings, there is virtually a phobia against any reminder of our pulse-driven past, a desperate avoidance of anything suggestive of the old bondage.

With the decline of periodic pulse as a structural matrix for music came unprecedented difficulties in performance. These arose from the fact that our notational system, and hence the training of performers, is largely based on progressive halving of a basic unit of time. Other fractional subdivisions on the one hand, and additive rhythms on the other, have had to be fitted into the procrustean notational system. The frequent result is the obfuscation, by the notation, of the underlying musical intention. Performance, in turn, suffers both from misunderstanding of the musical meaning, and from inaccuracies occasioned by the notational complexity.

One way out of the dilemma has been to make a virtue of a necessity and compose in such a way that "approximate" rhythmic performance is taken for granted. The composer then may notate rhythm precisely, expecting the performer to play it approximately, or he abandons conventional notation altogether and uses some form of analog notation, or as a third alternative employs some aleatoric device. All these approaches are, to a greater or lesser degree, limited in their ability to articulate molecular rhythmic structure. The architectural unit may be subatomic, or on the other hand, it may approximate the consistency of rubber, or even butter. The burden of this paper is to offer one approach to rhythm that, so to speak, permits throwing out the bath water while holding onto the baby.

Some years ago I had reasoned that if it were only possible to develop a means whereby performers could maintain complete independence as to tempo, meter, and positioning of the beat, and yet be precisely coordinated in time, a great deal stood to be gained. If in addition it were also possible to make frequent changes in any of these parameters while the ensemble remained precisely coordinated, we would be on our way to enjoying a resource for composition and performance which would permit taking advantage of pulse, either regular or aperiodic, where it was desired, and yet not in any way be hobbled by its freight of problems.

After much experimentation such a system has evolved and has been used in the performance of a number of works written especially to exploit its potential. In brief the system involves a magnetic tape recording on which signals to the individual performers have been pre-recorded at different pitch levels. A lightweight cable connects the tape playback unit to the performers, each of whom hears, through a miniature earphone, only those signals intended for him. The cable could easily be replaced by short-range radio transmission.

For purposes of detailed exposition it is convenient to break down the technical procedures into three categories:

1. Preparation of the score
2. Preparation of the audio signal tape
3. Communication system

1. *Preparation of the Score.* The first task is the preparation of what in effect is a conductor's schematic score, individualized for each part. Above each musical staff, then, is added the beat or signal structure pertaining to that instrument. The symbols used are borrowed directly

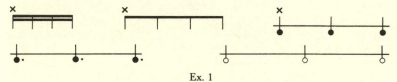

Ex. 1

from conventional notation and represent ♪, ♪, ♩, ♩., ♩ durations, respectively (See Ex. 1). Durational symbols that normally are beamed are for this purpose notated without heads ⊓, ♪, ⊓⊓. ; those that do not naturally have beams, now are given heads, centrally located so as to avoid confusion in alignment. In order to join groupings of notes that are not customarily beamed I have used a brace *through* the middle of the stem, extending beyond both ends of the grouplet. This scheme together with the use of an × over accented beats makes it possible to meaningfully relate the beat structure to the music.

Ex. 2   Ghent, *Dithyrambos*[1]

[1] In the interest of clarity a portion of the Horn part is omitted. Bass Trombone is tacet here.
[2] Tempo relations form a 4:3 progression: 94.8, 71.1, 53.3, 40, and later 30 (60/2) in the Bass Trombone, and 22.5 (90/4) in Trumpet II.

A work of complex rhythmic structure, if composed with this system in mind, will often appear quite straightforward on paper. Ex. 2 illustrates the beginning of a sequence of 3 : 4 augmentations, the standard notation of which would be formidable indeed. The Carter Double Concerto for Harpsichord and Piano (Ex. 3) provides a dramatic illustration of how different a score may appear when translated into multi-tempo notation. The individual parts in Ex. 3b present no difficulty to the performer and facilitate expression of the now explicit pulse when this is desired.

If a score is to be written with a beat structure in one common tempo, it of course need not be spatially proportionate. On the other hand, if multiple simultaneous tempi and beat staggerings are employed, the only way to indicate timing relationships is if the score is written to scale. Along with the interesting rhythmic possibilities afforded by this degree of tempo flexibility come a few necessary notational devices. Wherever there is a sudden change of tempo in one voice, a few preparatory beats at the new tempo may be required, unless the new tempo coincides with a long held note, in which case the performer accustoms himself to the new tempo while playing (Ex. 4: tempo change from $\quarternote = 100$ to $\quarternote = 84$). Here the 𝄖 at the new tempo enables the cellist to place the note accurately at the second $\quarternote$ of $\quarternote = 84$.

If tempo changes are not to inhibit one's freedom as to downbeat placement in the new tempo, another indicator is needed—a means of notating an indeterminate duration that is easily heard and learned, but is very cumbersome to notate. If the composer wishes both to have the high D of the cello part coincide with the γ in the violin, *and* to change to a new and only indirectly related tempo ($\quarternote = 84$), he is obliged to make use of some notational device to indicate what would otherwise be extremely awkward to notate. I have used the symbol W for a beat of indeterminate value (in this case $\mathsf{W} = \quarternote_{100} + \eighthnote_{84}$), and W for an actual note (in this case $\mathsf{W} = \wholenote_{100} + \eighthnote_{84}$). A rest of indeterminate duration is notated ⊟; a change in tempo by the symbol ∇; 𝄖 over any beat symbol indicates that a fast triple signal will be heard either as a checkpoint, or as an alerting cue just before the end of a long rest. Finally, since barlines have vanished and in any case would be independently located on each staff, some means of position reference, such as a time-track, is valuable. If the score has been made to a time scale, it is evident that the notation is at the same time conventional and proportional (analog). A convenient way of indicating rehearsal points is by 〉〉 through the entire system, thereby indicating to each performer exactly which beat he will hear first.

Ex. 3a, 3b. Carter, Double Concerto for Harpsichord and Piano
Ex. 3a. Mm. 12–16, as the original score but with proportionate spacing.
Ex. 3b. Identical section in multitempo notation, with beat structure indicated.

[1] In the interest of clarity all instruments other than percussion, and all markings other than those pertaining to rhythm have been omitted. Each line and space of each staff represents a separate percussion instrument.

[2] Although they are unessential, and in fact slightly misleading because of placement *before* a beat, barlines have been added in Ex. 3b to more clearly illustrate the metric regularities.

[3] Use of ♪+, ♩+, etc. A persistent problem in conventional notation results from a peculiarity in our symbolic counting language—1, 2, 3, 4, 3 + 2, 6, 7, 8 (e.g., ♪, ♪, ♪, ♩, ♩., ♩, ♩, ♩., ♩.., ♩). To fill the vacancy for 5 and thereby avoid the use of misleading ties, I have employed ♪+, ♩+, etc, where the + adds an extra 1/4 to the value of a duration, just as a dot adds an extra 1/2. Similarly an × would add 1/8 to the value, so that ♩× = ♪♪♪♪ or ♪♪♪♪♪ or ♪♪♪♪♪♪ or ♩ ♩+ ♩+ ♩+

[4] ▽ indicates new tempo.

[5] Unless otherwise indicated, ♪ = ♪ on any given staff.

· 138 ·

Ex. 4

2. *Preparation of Audio Signal Tape.* Once the signal structure, including accents, alerting cues and rehearsal points for the entire piece has been worked out, it must now be translated into audio signals on magnetic tape. Up to the present this has been accomplished with the aid of the coordinome,[2] essentially a punched tape reading device. There are four steps involved in translating the schematic beat structure of the piece into the final audio signal tape.

1. Assigning a real time value to every signal in the piece.
2. Transferring this data to punched IBM cards.
3. Automatic conversion from punched cards to punched tape.
4. Conversion of punched tape into the multiplexed audio magnetic tape.

Calculating the real time value of all the signals is a clerical chore involving the use of a desk calculator, or for the most part, an adding machine. The transfer of these data to punched cards is likewise a clerical task, either for a key-punch operator, or an assistant to mark and punch IBM cards (e.g., the 40-character per card Port-a-Punch card). A printed grid on each card indicates 1 card = 40 characters = 1 second, so that each 4 characters = 100 msec. After assigning each of eight horizontal tracks to represent one signal channel, the timing data are now entered on the cards. A single hole punched at the appropriate place will result in a single beat signal of .025 sec. (1/40 sec.) duration. Four consecutive punched holes will produce a signal sounding much louder rather than longer, and will be the means of indicating an accented beat, ✕. The alerting or checkpoint signal 𝍍 will be punched as -x-x-x-. Rehearsal points may be punched in as a single hole in one of the 8 tracks designated for this purpose. Once the entire deck of cards has been marked and punched, the cards are machine-converted to punched tape on a hole for hole basis. If the punched tape is now run

---

[2] The coordinome was designed and developed at New York University by the author and Stein G. Raustein. For further details, see Emmanuel Ghent, "The Coordinome in Relation to Electronic Music," *Electronic Music Review,* Vol. 1, No. 1 (1967), pp. 33–43.

through the coordinome at 40 characters per second (4 i.p.s.),[3] the holes will gate the input signal to all 8 channels at the absolute tempi indicated in the score. Running the machine faster or slower will result in a corresponding change in overall tempo; the constituent tempi will, of course, remain in constant relation to each other. An early version of this signalling system used a white noise input common to all channels. This was gated by the coordinome and differentially distributed to the performers by a multiple conductor cable. In order to obviate the need of the coordinome itself at rehearsals or performance, the present system was devised wherein each signal channel has its own sinusoidal input at a specified frequency. The separate outputs are then mixed and recorded on a single track of magnetic tape. For ease of subsequent decoding it is convenient to use frequencies at half octave intervals, 250, 350, 500, 700, 1000, hz., etc.

The multiplexed signal tape may be regarded as an extremely simple electronic composition in which there are no more than 8 pitches, all at the same dynamic level, only 2 note durations, and the relation among attack points, while often complex, is still very simple relative to the piece of music for which it constitutes the beat structure. Viewed from this perspective, digital computer synthesis of the tape immediately suggests itself as an alternative to the coordinome-based procedure. Indeed, George Logemann has worked out a computer program that creates, from the beat structure time data, the appropriate digitalized waveforms which then may be converted to analog signals by using a digital-to-analog converter.[4] He is also developing a symbolic notation, closely related to musical language, which will enable the composer to communicate, via a typewriter, with the computer.[5] Output will take the form either of the fully synthesized audio tape or the appropriately punched paper tape for use with the coordinome.

Regardless of how the audio tape is prepared, markers[6] must be attached to it at suitable points, so that any rehearsal point may be quickly and precisely located visually by the tape recorder operator. For purposes of rehearsal it is often desirable to prepare a second audio tape similar in all details, but recorded below tempo.

[3] Likewise, an 80-character card could be used, yielding 8 characters per 100 msec. The punched tape would then be run through the coordinome at 80 characters/sec. or 8 inches/sec.

[4] The work on digital music synthesis is being conducted by Benjamin Boretz, Richard Friedman, Robert Laupheimer, and George Logemann, under the auspices of the Engineering Research Laboratory of the Courant Institute of Mathematical Sciences, and the Institute for Computer Research in the Humanities, both of New York University. Recently, with the assistance of Hubert S. Howe Jr., a signal tape was prepared using the music 4B program.

[5] Cf. George Logemann, "A Symbolic Notation for Electronic Music Synthesis," to appear in a forthcoming issue of the *Electronic Music Review*.

[6] For this purpose yellow lay-out tape (3/16" x 3¼") is attached to the surface of the magnetic tape and appropriately marked. An opaque colored tape of the thinness of splicing tape would be preferable.

3. *Communication System.* The communication system consists of a driver unit, a length of lightweight cable, the decoder units, and miniature earphones. The output of the tape-reproduce pre-amplifier is fed through the driver unit (amplifier and power supply for the filter decoders),[7] and thence via the cable to the performers. The cable may have to be 150' long in order to extend from backstage, especially if performers are to be positioned off-stage. At periodic intervals along the cable there are outlets into any one of which the performer plugs his earphone-decoder unit (about the size of a transistor radio).

The Signal System in Relation to the Composer

A further application of the signal system lies in its use as a means of synchronizing electronic tape music with live performers. The impossibility up to the present of effecting precise synchronization has made it necessary for composers to employ a variety of devices to compensate for this limitation. The present system makes it possible to synchronize precisely with performers over the entire duration of the piece. This was accomplished in *Hex, an Ellipsis for Trumpet, Instruments and Tape,* by using one of four tracks on 1/2" magnetic tape for signals to the performers, and the other three tracks for electronically generated music. The synchronization is done in the studio as the final step in the composition.

In writing for the larger chamber ensembles, or when using still larger symphonic forces, it would be impractical to have each musician on a separate signal channel. Two alternatives remain. The composer may elect to assign a group of 2, 3, or more instruments to a given signal channel. With very large ensembles, however, it will probably turn out more useful to divide the orchestra into smaller units each of which has a separate conductor. The conductors now, rather than the performers, are synchronized by the signal system.

Although there have been experiments in the use of wide spatial separation of performers or orchestral subgroups, the problem of adequate ensemble playing has plagued such ventures. The present signal system is well suited to antiphonal purposes, as it makes possible virtually any placement of performers.

To the composer the signal system is nothing more than a technical resource that must be adapted to his own purposes. One may write in such a way as to make the signals an integral part of the work; or one may conceive of it purely as a rehearsal aid. One composer may make frequent use of multiple tempi, another may prefer to write in a common tempo but make use of conflicting rhythmic constellations that

[7] To ensure complete channel-separation of signals, a limiting amplifier is included in the decoder unit. The filter attenuates all signals other than those at the desired frequency, and the limiting amplifier amplifies only those signals above a certain dynamic level. The net result is a complete elimination of unwanted signals.

would be very difficult to realize accurately without some coordinating device. On one occasion, multiple tempi may function primarily to evoke the sense of tension among several pulses, on another to emphasize resultant rhythms among discrete pulses, or on still another to exploit the possibilities of asynchronous attack points, or of a pulseless flux.

Instead of being bound by the classical system of binary diminutions (2^n), a composer may wish to work with diminutions or augmentations of a $3:2$, $4:3$, $5:3$, or other ratio $[(3/2)^n, (4/3)^n, (5/3)^n,$ etc., respectively]. Conventional notation will barely sustain two levels of diminution of a $(3/2)^n$ relationship $[3/2)^2$, or $9:4]$. Beyond this the notation becomes extremely cumbersome and performance seriously compromised. If, however, the music is composed using multiple tempi and a signal system employed to ensure accuracy, the difficulty vanishes.[8]

To be sure, there are new problems created by multiple tempo compositions, such as how to arrange for rhythmic unisons at points called for by musical considerations rather than by mathematical coincidence. As with other such difficulties simple solutions are readily at hand, in this case by interposing a single beat of "indeterminate" duration (⩔) at a suitable location.

Not infrequently a composer clearly hears a rhythmic structure which, when tapped out, may be easily imitated. However, when it is accurately notated, and the performer comes to play it, great difficulty is experienced in accurately rendering the composer's intention. In *Hex,* the rhythmic figure of Ex. 5 appears in which each note is played by a different instrument. When notated so as to eliminate the ties,[9] and the performers are given an advance cue of the exact rhythmic pattern expected, little difficulty arises in execution. In effect, a periodic pulse has been replaced by a predictable but aperiodic pulse that is both seen and heard by the musicians.

(♩ = 100)

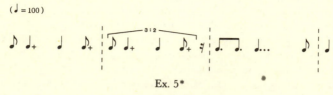

Ex. 5*

Objection has been raised that the inexorable beat would allow none of the ebb and flow, the slight rubati that in earlier music was essential to the musical value of the piece. Apart from the obvious fact that much

[8] Cf. Ex. 2.

[9] See footnote 3 to Ex. 3.

* The ⌐——3:2——⌐ segment repeats the preceding four note figure but at 3/2 tempo (27 ♪ in the time of 18 ♪).

new music derives its rhythmic interest and meaning from devices very different from those of a previous era, it is important to note that if so desired, rubati, accelerandi, etc., may in fact be included by at least three different means: (1) by deliberately using a very slow regular beat as a scaffolding around which the performer is asked to weave freely according to an essentially spatial notation; (2) by composing an accelerando into the beat durations themselves; (3) by composing giusto, and then creating the accelerando "by ear" when converting the punched tape into the multiplexed audio tape.

Signal System in Relation to Performers and Conductors

Experience over three years has made it apparent that performers adapt very quickly to the use of the miniature earphone.[10] In general they have found the signals extremely helpful in rehearsal and perform-ance. In the first rehearsal the tendency is for the musician to hew strictly to his own part. As familiarity develops both with the piece and with the technique, the sense of ensemble returns. Rehearsal time is enormously reduced as rhythmic problems have virtually disappeared, and the full attention of the ensemble can be directed to interpretive as-pects of the music. To this end a conductor is invaluable. Freed from the necessity of directing most of his energies to being a time-keeper, the conductor is able to devote himself to the expressive and structural as-pects of the music.

The Coordinome in Relation to Electronic Music Synthesis

Such are the ways of serendipity that the coordinome turned out to have an application entirely unrelated to the signal distribution system. Through the inventiveness of Robert Moog, of Trumansburg, New York, the coordinome is now being utilized, in conjunction with a bank of voltage-controlled sound generating and modifying equipment, as a syn-thesizer of electronic music.[11] The punched tape reader mechanism, in-stead of gating audio signals as described in the previous system, is now used to control the sound generating equipment. Using simple binary codes for programming quantized increments of the input voltage to os-cillators, amplifiers, band-pass filters, frequency modulators, envelope generators, etc., a rather elaborate system of planned electronic music

[10] Lejaren A. Hiller at the University of Illinois is currently developing a system similar to that described in this paper. One difference will be the use of visual (opaque lights) in place of auditory stimuli.

[11] The electronic moieties of *Hex* were in large measure synthesized by this procedure.

Somewhat similar systems, employing direct computer output rather than the intermedia-tion of punched paper tape, have been developed at the University of Illinois by Lejaren A. Hiller, and at the University of Toronto by Gustav Ciamaga. The coordinome-paper-tape approach permits extensive compositional trials without tying up the computer for hours at a time. For the details of this system, see Emmanuel Ghent, *op. cit.*

synthesis is made possible. Other functions, as for example, selection of waveform, or choice of output channel, may be performed with the use of simple logic circuits. Speeds up to 100 notes, or other musical events, per second are possible with simple programming, and up to 20–25 events per second with elaborate programming.

This system differs in many respects both from digital computer synthesis, and from electronic music synthesis involving the use of a sequencer. It uniquely affords the opportunity for *both* programmed control, *and* manual influence in real time. Manipulable operations on a given segment of punched tape include transposition, literal inversion or retrograding, continuous speed variation (over a 10:1 range) without affecting pitch, compression or expansion of pitch ratios, variations in center-frequency and band-width of a pass-band (while the *relation* of these variables from note to note remains, of course, a function of the original programming), variations in timbre by adding harmonic, subharmonic, or non-harmonic partials, variations in envelope, and so on. In contrast to the sequencer, each musical event may be uniquely programmed with regard to a variety of parameters. Furthermore, there is virtually no limit to the total number of such events in any given sequence. Time relations among the musical events are a direct function of distance on the paper tape.

As indicated earlier in the performer-coordinating system, there are a variety of approaches to the preparation of the paper tape. Here too, the most elegant is through the agency of a computer. George Logemann[12] is preparing a program whereby the composer will be able to communicate with the computer in essentially musical language, yielding output in the form of perforated paper tape and/or direct control of the sound generating equipment.[13] An added advantage of no little significance is that a small computer is quite sufficient for this purpose, in contrast to the giants required for digital music synthesis.

[12] See footnote 5, above.

See George Logemann, "Automated Techniques for Programmed Electronic Music Synthesis," *Electronic Music Review*, Vol. 1, No. 1 (1967), pp. 44–53.

[13] As a third alternative, output in the form of digitalized waveforms will be available for conversion to the analog signal. See footnote 2 above.

1967

ON VIOLIN HARMONICS

PAUL ZUKOFSKY

I N T H E technique of violin playing few areas are as unclear as that of har-monics. That an easily accessible, standardized, and current chart of the many harmonics is not available to composers is one side of the problem. The fact is that when a composer goes to a violinist for a fingering and is told that there is only one way to produce a certain resultant sound (and most violinists do not really know the possibilities of their instrument) he accepts this as authority, even though the choice may have no relation to the ease with which a whole passage can be played. This lack of knowledge on the violinist's part is certainly more distressing than the composer's guess. I hope that what follows will help clear up this general fogginess, both for composer and performer.

There are two types of string harmonics—natural and artificial. A natural harmonic is the pitch (resultant) that is produced by lightly touching an open, vibrating string (the fundamental) at one of the nodes located at 1/2, 1/3, 1/4, etc. the length of the string. An artificial harmonic is a harmonic whose fundamental must be artificially created by stopping (shortening) the string to the desired fundamental. This is done by pressing strongly with a lower finger (usually the first, except in the case of third harmonics or fourth harmonics using an extension fingering—the latter being uncommon), and then obtaining the resultant by touching lightly with a higher finger one of the nodes at 1/2, etc. the length of the shortened string. This artificiality of the fundamental is one of three characteristics that differentiate natural from artificial harmonics.

The resultants that we hear are, of course, the partials of the funda-mental. The first through fifth partials are the only resultants that are used. Partials higher than these are almost totally unreliable because of the small distance involved in their fingering, and because the intervallic ratios of the harmonic series are not easily combined with the unclear system of violin intonation (which, whatever that is based on, does not take into consideration the small number ratios of the harmonic series). These small number ratios are already a problem with the fourth and fifth partial, but more of that later. In the set of all the possible natural har-monics excited from one fundamental, we find that many of the resultants can be produced at more than one place on the string. This is because of the division of the string in the harmonic series into small number ratios. There is an ordering of partials up to the mid-point on the string (octave) and from there the same ordering in retrograde from octave to bridge. This duplication of resultants is impossible in a set of artificial harmonics excited from one fundamental, because the four fingers used for pitches on the violin can barely stretch the octave on one string—(equal to a twelfth on adjacent strings). This non-duplication of resultants is another distinguishing mark of the artificial harmonic, and the possibility of vibrating the fundamental is the third characteristic. Generally, all natural harmonics have a "purer" sound than artificial ones, though if the artificial fundamental is well stopped, much of its impurity disappears.

Since we have determined above that all possible different harmonics of one fundamental fall within the span of one octave, let us convert these small number ratios into intervals up to the octave. Consequently, harmonics occur at the lightly touched octave, fifth, fourth, major and minor third, and major sixth. The last is of no use since the stretch (equal to a major tenth) is not always secure, and the range of the major sixth harmonic is exactly that of the major third. The touched octave, whose resultant is an octave higher than the fundamental, is another matter. While the stretch is greater than that of the major sixth, it is the only way to produce the resultants below d—4th line—treble clef (see Ex. 1). The first of these, being a natural harmonic, needs no restrictions. The others

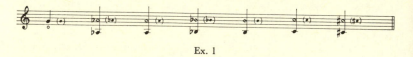

Ex. 1

must be used with extreme care; one must give a reasonable amount of time to prepare the stretch, and not require it to be held too long. This word of caution is due to the fact that some violinists' hands cannot possibly make the reach, regardless of the amount of preparation, and for those who can it is not yet common practice to go flying all over the fingerboard and land on an artificial harmonic. The maximum dynamic level of an artificial octave harmonic is not loud. The sound is rather throaty and tremulous, but could be made use of. Above the range indicated below, the artificial octave harmonic is superfluous.

The resultant of the touched fifth is one octave and a fifth higher than the fundamental (Ex. 2). The touched fourth gives a resultant two octaves higher than the fundamental (Ex. 3). The touched major third's resultant

Ex. 2

Ex. 3

Ex. 4

is two octaves and a major third higher than the fundamental, and the minor third gives a resultant two octaves and a fifth above the fundamental (Ex. 4). It is with these two types of third harmonics that we run into the problems of the small number ratios mentioned above. As is probably clear by now, when we talk of small number ratios in the harmonic series, we are referring to the "just" intervals, in this case the just major third of 4:5, and the just minor third of 5:6. The 5:6 minor third is 316 cyclic cents wide (16 cents sharper than the equal tempered minor third of 300 cents), and the 4:5 major third is 386 cents wide (14 cents flatter than the equal tempered major third). This means that the distance between the 4:5 and 5:6 third is only 70 cyclic cents. This makes a rather small semitone as opposed to the equal semitone of 100 cents. Consequently, while one of these thirds must be flattened, and the other sharpened (otherwise they will not speak), one must be cautious not to overdo either correction as it may result in the breaking of one resultant to another. This is the main reason that third harmonics, especially minor third harmonics, are not always used by violinists. However, the delicacy of touch required in third harmonics is quite possible and provides an invaluable technical resource in passages of quickly changing harmonics over a wide range. They are also indispensable in double harmonics.

Generally, if a violin player is not secure in third harmonics it is best for him to switch to a fourth or fifth harmonic, until he learns the technique of handling thirds. There are no restrictions on the fourth and fifth harmonics; both have large dynamic range, and the fifth is slightly purer than the fourth. Both fourth and fifth are purer than third harmonics, which do not have quite the dynamic range of the former. With all these cautions about third harmonics, I would still prefer them to awkward string changes, as with good touch and an incisive attack from the bow these disadvantages can be minimized.

Double harmonics are two harmonics played simultaneously on adjacent strings. They may be either two natural harmonics, two artificial harmonics, or one natural and one artificial harmonic. Both harmonics should be either in the same position or in adjacent half-step positions. It is possible to play double harmonics with three or even two fingers. In that case one finger either stops both fundamentals, or touches both nodes. The same finger cannot stop a fundamental on one string, and touch a node on the other. The dynamic of these double harmonics depends considerably on the bow stroke. Another type of double stop possible is that of combining a regular note with a harmonic on an adjacent string. The above restrictions on fingering still apply. These types of double stops are quite possible, though they are a problem in terms of bow stroke. It is not necessary here to go into exact detail regarding bow strokes for this type of double stop. Let it suffice that one must be cautious of overplaying the real note, as it will automatically be louder than the harmonic.

The chart of the various harmonics is read as follows: reading vertically will give you all the possible ways to produce a given resultant; horizontally, the top staff gives resultants, and the staffs numbered 1–10 are half-step increments in ascending positions along the violin fingerboard. The 0 staff gives the natural harmonics, which are not as position-bound as the artificial ones. The numerals I, II, III, and IV, signify respectively E, A, D, and G strings. The procedure for determining a fingering for two successive harmonics is as follows: locate both resultants, and then find the choices that are closest to each other horizontally, and involve the same or adjacent strings. (See pp. 149–52.)

A word about notation. Only natural octave harmonics should be written with a round note head and a small zero above the note. All other harmonics should be written with diamonds. All harmonics should have the resultant indicated in parenthesis next to the harmonic. This small effort insures that the right note will be played by the performer even if he cannot use the composer's fingering. If one especially desires a particular timbral quality, the string should be indicated. In actuality, however, timbral differentiation is minimized among strings now that all four strings are available with aluminum winding, though in very high positions, on sustained notes, timbral variation is still easily perceptible (i.e., between a minor third harmonic high on the D string or on the A string and the same resultant produced on the E string with a fifth harmonic).

1968

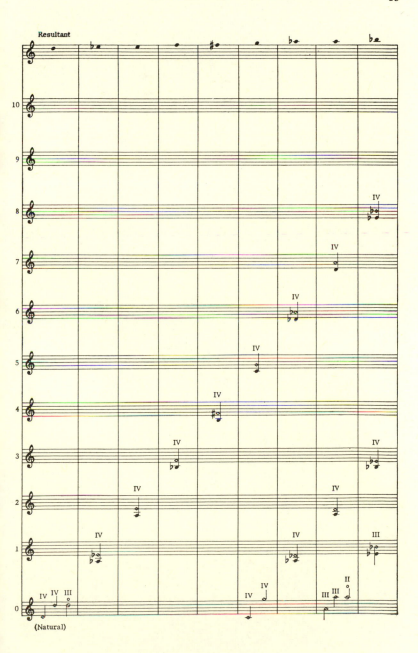

Resultant
10 IV IV III
9 IV IV III
8 IV III IV
7 IV III IV
6 IV III IV
5 IV III IV IV III
4 IV III IV IV III
3 III IV IV III II
2 III IV IV III II
1 IV IV III II III
0 IV IV IV IV IV III IV III II II I III III III III
(Natural)

Resultant

(Natural)

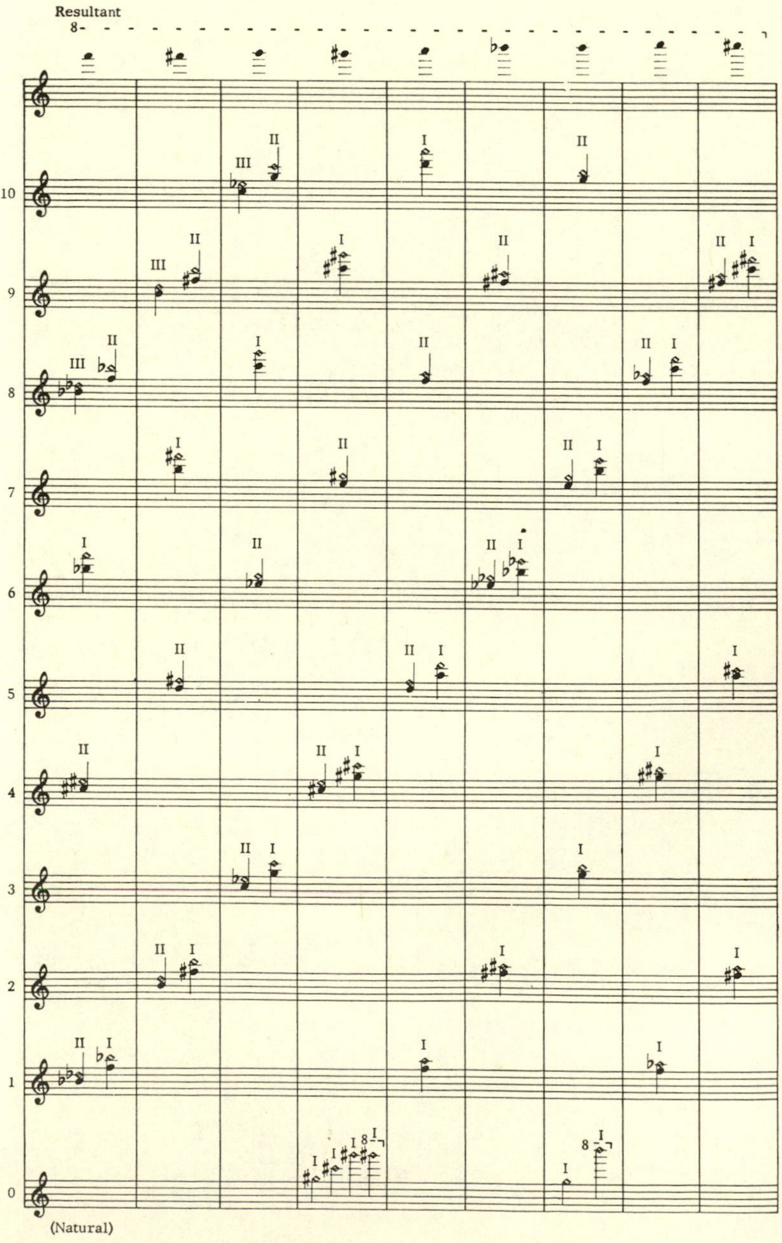
Resultant
8
10
9
8
7
6
5
4
3
2
1
0
(Natural)

GRAPHICAL LANGUAGE FOR THE SCORES OF COMPUTER-GENERATED SOUNDS

M. V. MATHEWS and L. ROSLER

I. Introduction

THE VALUE of digital computers for generating sound and for simulating speech transmission devices has been well established [1,2,3,4]. Existing programs produce a large variety of sounds using programmed instruments which simulate real instruments or are wholly artificial. Simple computer languages [5] allow each composer to construct his own unique instruments quickly and easily.

However, specifying the sounds to be produced by these programs can be time-consuming. Usually the parameters specifying each sound or note are punched on a computer card. At least five numbers—the instrument to be played, the starting time, duration, frequency, and amplitude—are necessary to specify a single note. Although punching individual note cards is a usable composing process, possibilities for improvement exist— possibilities based on better methods of man-computer communication. This paper discusses one such approach using a graphic-input computer, the Graphic 1 [6].

The Graphic 1 allows a person to enter pictures and graphs directly into a computer memory by the very act of drawing these objects. Moreover, the power of the computer is available to modify, erase, duplicate, and remember the drawings. A graphical composition language has been invented which allows the score of a piece to be specified as a group of graphs; thus the full power of the Graphic 1 can be applied to the act of composing.

Experiments with graphic scores had already been made by such well-known composers as Varèse, Stockhausen, and Grainger. Hence, this form of score promised to be both readily developed and powerful. In addition to fulfilling these promises, the scores provided a means of enlisting the computer to aid the composer. Useful algorithms could be written, by means of which the computer generates parts of the music.

The Graphic 1 computer was intended as an aid to engineering designers. It has been applied to a variety of design problems, from electric circuits to mechanical objects. Designers must specify the details of many interacting parts. Often, individual parts are simple, but their interaction is complex. The overall operation of the device must be kept in mind while one is concentrating on the details of a particular part.

Viewed in this light, a musical composition is a typical design problem. The overall structure of the piece must not be forgotten while one is working on the details of a section. The main auditory effects arise from the interactions of many notes which are individually simple.

The Graphic 1 has proven to be a powerful tool for design problems. It is possible to sketch the outlines of objects and fill in the details later. Sometimes the computer can provide the details by means of an algorithm. These design techniques, developed for engineering purposes, may benefit composers as well. In addition, its application to computer music may aid the development of machine-aided engineering design. Computer sounds have the unique advantage of being not only designable but also manufacturable on a computer. Thus, the finished product is immediately available for evaluation and possible redesign. Such rapid feedback is an ideal laboratory in which to develop design procedures.

The rest of the paper presents the details of the graphical scores and algorithms. Section II reviews the operation of the Graphic 1 computer. Section III discusses the special computer language which adapts the Graphic 1 to the design of compositions. The representation of sound sequences by graphs and the composition algorithms are presented in Section IV. (The Appendix gives a complete list of the available graphic statements.)

II. The Interaction System

System Organization

The heart of the system is the MUSIC IV program for the IBM 7094 (Ex. 1, right) [3,4,5]. The input to this program is normally a sequence of symbolic "note" cards, each of which specifies the simulated instrument to be played, the starting time and duration of a note, its amplitude and frequency, and other parameters. The output of the program is a digital magnetic tape consisting of sequential amplitude samples of the generated sound.

In the past, it has been necessary to specify the note cards in detail. The graphical language to be described allows the note cards to be generated *by a computer program*, from simpler data specified in terms of functions which vary with time in a piecewise linear manner, and combinations of these functions. While the composer visualizes these functions as two-dimensional graphs, the actual input to the graphical-score translator

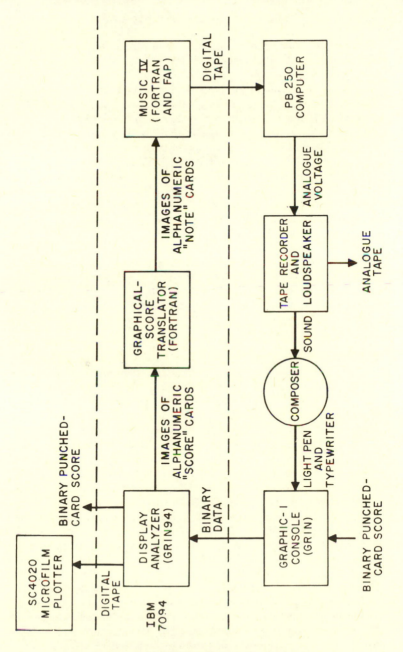

Ex. 1. Block Diagram of Complete Sound Generating Loop

(Ex. 1, center) consists of card images consisting of alphanumeric data (the coordinates of the vertices of the graphs, and other numerical descriptors).

The next step in simplification is the introduction of a graphical-input system (Ex. 1, left), whose ultimate purpose is to perform the tedious clerical task of reducing the two-dimensional graphs drawn by the composer to the symbolic data cards required by the graphical-score translator. The Graphic 1 console, a computer system with real-time graphical input and display facilities, makes the production and editing of the music functions by the composer a relatively simple and convenient job. It should be stressed, however, that alternatively the sound-generating programs in the 7094 computer can be addressed directly by hand-punched "score" cards, as was in fact done before the Graphic 1 console was used.

The output link to the composer, which closes the man-machine interaction loop, consists of the actual sound sequence generated from his graphical input. The digital tape produced by MUSIC IV is rewound and transmitted to another computer (PB250; Ex. 1, right), which converts the amplitude samples into an analogue voltage. The voltage is filtered, recorded on magnetic tape, and transmitted to the composer via an amplifier and a loud-speaker. Monoaural or stereophonic output may be requested by the composer.

The Graphic 1 Console

The Graphic 1 console is a small computer system equipped with a light pen for graphical input, a typewriter keyboard for alphanumeric input, a card reader for binary input, and a cathode-ray tube for graphical output. Typewriter output is used only for debugging or error messages. The console is "dedicated" to the composer during the course of a composing session and interacts as necessary with the IBM 7094. It would not be economical for the 7094 to be continuously accessible, waiting idly during the composer's thinking time. Instead the 7094 runs other jobs between the composer's uses.

The console consists of a DEC PDP-5 computer, a DEC 340 cathode-ray-tube oscilloscope, an Ampex RVQ buffer memory, and appropriate hardware interfaces (Ex. 2). The information stored in the Ampex consists primarily of instructions which may be decoded to create a display on the face of the cathode-ray tube. In addition, the Ampex can store non-display data, for example encoded descriptions of the various displayable elements.

The name of the light pen is deceptive. It is not a light-generating device, but rather a light-sensing device—in fact, a shutter-equipped flexible fiber-optics tube connected to a photocell in the computer cabinet. The photocell signals the computer when it detects light, and the coordinates of the cathode-ray-tube beam at that time can be recorded by the program.

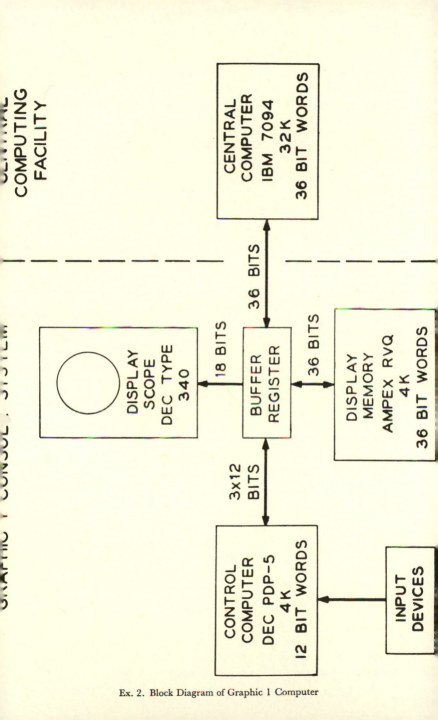

Ex. 2. Block Diagram of Graphic 1 Computer

The GRIN (GRaphical INput) language [7] for the Graphic 1 console includes two commands by means of which data can be supplied by the light pen: to answer the questions *where* and *which*.

To answer the question *where*, a tracking cross is displayed sixty times a second. The program attempts to keep the cross centered in the field of view of the light pen. The cross thus allows positional information to be conveyed to the program even where nothing is being displayed.

To answer the question *which*, the operator points the light pen at an entity displayed on the screen such as, for example, a word of text. The program determines the entity being pointed at and causes it to be intensified, thus providing visual feedback to confirm the operator's choice. The program can then take alternative actions depending on which entity is selected by the operator.

The oscilloscope thus serves three functions: selective display of the contents of the Ampex memory; a drawing surface for use with the light pen; and a control surface on which various control segments may be displayed, with mnemonic shapes or labels supplied by the programmer. These so-called "light buttons," when pointed at by the light pen, cause entry to specific subprograms. As the light buttons are tailored to fit the problem to be solved, they constitute a problem-oriented language, the only computer-control language which the composer need learn. This use of the display surface for control has many advantages: the attention of the operator need not be diverted from the display; the display is flexible, so only those control functions which are meaningful at the moment are presented to the operator; appropriate messages can be displayed to the operator to direct him to supply data as required by the various subprograms. Thus the program itself instructs the composer in its own use.

III. The Graphical-Input Programs

The Graphic 1 GRIN Program

The GRIN program used for the generation of graphical scores divides the display surface into two areas: a region for light buttons and messages to the composer, and a grid on which the music functions are drawn.

Example 3 is a view reproduced from microfilm of the blank display surface seen by the composer. A microfilm of the display is automatically provided each time the composer interacts with the IBM 7094. These microfilms provide an essential record of the score. The examples given in this paper are all prepared from these microfilms.

The abscissa of the grid is duration either in beats or in arbitrary units proportional to time. Standard scales for pitch or loudness are provided for the ordinate; non-standard scales can be specified by the composer, as will be discussed later. The grid is included in all the microfilm output

FUNCTN   NØTES   CØPYALL CØMMENT DELETE   MØVE   7094   LØAD   CLEAR   FRAME   A

                 CØPY FN   RETYPE   ØVERLAY   L

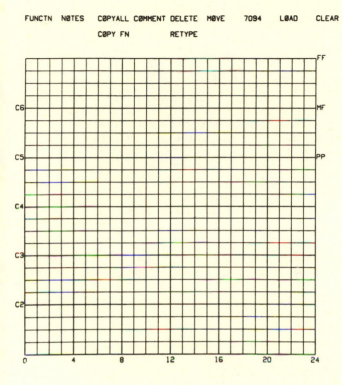

Ex. 3. Blank Frame of Score

generated by the 7094. For clarity of presentation in this paper, the minor grid structure has been suppressed in later figures by a temporary modification of the program.

The light buttons and their operations are listed in the Appendix. We shall describe here the typical way the buttons are used. Information comprising the score consists of graphic functions, drawn on the grid with line segments, followed by a line of text consisting of a three-letter label followed by two or more numerical parameters.

The FUNCTN button is used to draw most of the functions. Because of the self-explanatory nature of light buttons and the liberal use of messages to the user, which are displayed on the scope, the process can be learned with little effort.

When the light pen is pointed at the FUNCTN button, a tracking cross appears, and the light buttons are replaced by a message telling the composer to move the cross to the starting point of the function, which he indicates by pushing a button when the cross is positioned to his satisfaction. A temporary vector then appears, joining the tracking cross to the starting point with a "rubber-band" effect. A new message tells the composer to fix the successive vertices of the function permanently by pushing the button each time the cross is properly positioned. The composer completes the function by pushing a second button. He is then asked to type a line of descriptive text. The program then asks the composer to indicate (via the light pen on a new set of light buttons) whether any typing errors have been made. If so, he must retype the descriptor; if not, the main light buttons are displayed again and a new command may be initiated.

Other light buttons permit copying, deleting, and moving functions. Another asks for an interaction with the IBM 7094 to play a completed score. Another loads punched cards containing a previously drawn score in machine-readable form into the Graphic 1 memory.

The graphical score may be written onto any one of twelve frames. A particular frame is displayed on the scope by a light button. A second frame may then be overlayed on the scope face; in this way frames can be compared and functions copied from one frame into another.

The 7094 GRIN94 Program

The 7094 program that interacts with the Graphic 1 console is written in GRIN94 [8], a development of GRIN. The input consists solely of the contents of the Graphic 1 memory, i.e., the display which the composer has generated. Each frame in sequence is scanned for music functions. When a music function is found, the coordinates of its vertices are written sequentially onto a magnetic-disk file, followed by the typed descriptor of the function. This file is then presented as input to the graphical-score translator program.

In addition, a hard-copy permanent score is created by reproducing on microfilm each of the twelve frames which contains at least one music function, together with its identifying frame letter and the date and time of the interaction. A permanent copy of the graphical score in compact computer-readable form is also generated. This is a binary deck which may later be reloaded into the Graphic 1 or the 7094, and edited and reprocessed by the composer. This permits the composer to resume an interrupted session, from the point of the most recent interaction, without having to regenerate all his input manually.

IV. Specification of Sound Sequences and Music

How can the graphical facilities which have been described be used for the description of sound sequences? We shall first describe the simple representation of a sequence of sounds by graphic functions; then we shall describe some special procedures for composing with these functions. These composing algorithms are some of the most interesting results of the graphical language.

Simple Specification of Sound Sequences

The essential features of the method for specifying sound sequences can best be brought out by going through a few examples. A more detailed specification of the graphic language is in the Appendix. One form of the score for the first four measures (eight beats) of the march "The British Grenadiers" is shown in Ex. 4. Four functions are required, which specify amplitude, frequency, note durations, and any glissando (continuously changing frequency) which may be used. The conventional music score for this fragment is shown in Ex. 5 for comparison. On the graphic score two abscissa units equal one beat.

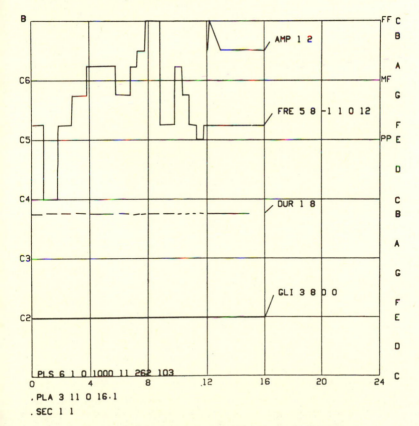

Ex. 4. Graphical Score for Fragment of "The British Grenadiers"

Ex. 5. Conventional Score for Fragment of "The British Grenadiers"

The upper function describes amplitude and is labeled AMP. The standard scale for amplitude is indicated along the upper right margin of the graph going from PP to FF. This particular function puts an accent on the first half-beat of each measure and plays the rest of the measure at a uniform amplitude. The "1" following the label AMP is a count indicating that one additional number is to follow. The "2" indicates that the function is two beats long. All functions are periodic and are repeated as many times as is appropriate. A non-periodic function may be constructed by using only one period of a periodic function. The positioning of the drawing from beats 12 to 16 on the abscissa has no significance; the periodic function will start at the beginning each time it is used.

The frequency function is shown immediately below the amplitude function and is labeled FRE. The normal frequency scale is shown on the left-hand side of the graph, C4 being the fourth C on the piano (middle C), C5 being an octave above, C3 being an octave below, and so forth. The numerical value of the frequency ordinate is equal to the logarithm to the base 2 of the ratio of the frequency to middle C (262 Hz). Thus C4 is zero, C5 is $+1$, etc. For this particular composition a more expanded diatonic scale is appropriate, which has been labeled along the right-hand side C, D, E. . . . These labels, written with the COMMENT light-button, are for the composer's benefit only. The program ignores them. Five numbers are written after the count following FRE. The 8 indicates that the duration of the function is eight beats. The correspondence between beats and time is made by a standard metronome marking not shown, the particular piece being played at a rate of 110 beats per minute. The -1 and 1 label the bottom and top of the graph, -1 corresponding to C an octave below middle C and 1 corresponding to C an octave above middle C, thus establishing the scale on the right. The 0 following the 1 is not used in this example. The 12 is an arbitrary number labeling the function for future reference in the algebra and also is not used here. In general, it is necessary to type only the numbers which differ from the standard scales built into the program. Thus if we had drawn the frequency function in terms of the standard scale on the left we could simply have written FRE 1 8.

Note durations are shown as a dashed line, the beginning of each dash denoting the beginning of the note, the end of the dash the end of the note. Glissando is not used in this composition and has been eliminated by making the frequency range of the glissando go from 0 to 0. When glissando is used, the logarithm of the frequency of each note is the value of the FRE function sampled at the beginning of the note plus the value of the glissando function generated as a continuous function of time.

Three typed statements appear at the bottom of the graph. (There are null functions associated with these statements; the functions are unused and invisible.) PLA requests that the computer play this score on instrument 11 from beat 0 to beat 16.1. Since the span to beat 16.1 is about twice the duration of the FRE and DUR functions, two repetitions of the four-measure sections will be produced by this demand.

The PLS statement requests a subroutine to quantize the note frequencies so they fall exactly on the even-tempered F major scale. In this way any small errors in drawing the FRE function will be eliminated. The details of the pitch quantizing will be discussed later.

The line labeled SEC terminates this section of the composition. The

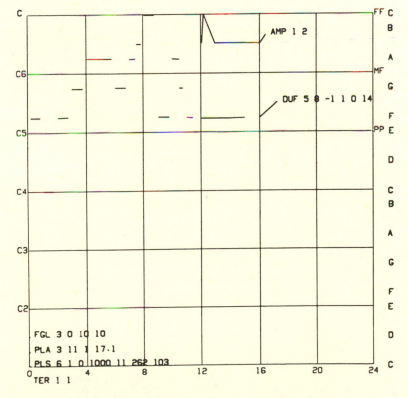

Ex. 6. Alternate Graphical Score for Fragment of "The British Grenadiers"

scores are all divided into sections, each of which starts at beat 0 and lasts until the last note called upon by any play instruction is completed.

An alternative, more compact and intuitive specification of the same score is shown on Ex. 6, the principal difference being that the frequency and durational functions have been combined into a single function labeled DUF. Frequencies are read as the ordinate to the DUF function, durations as the abscissa. The glissando function has not been drawn out but specified by an algebraic statement FGL which says that the glissando shall be calculated as the sum of function 10 plus function 10. Function 10, one of two standard functions built into the program, is identically zero, so glissando is eliminated. The details of the algebra, of which FGL is an example, will be elaborated in the next section. The other statements are similar to those of Ex. 4. The PLA plays two cycles of the composition starting at beat 1; hence there will be a one-beat rest at the beginning of the section which will separate it from the end of the previous section. The entire composition is ended by the TER statement.

Algebra for Combining Functions

The direct graphical specification of sound sequences described above is a simpler, faster, and surer method for putting this information into a computer than punching the equivalent numbers on computer cards. However, many additional features have been added to the graphical language. One of these is an algebra for combining graphical functions, which is especially useful for computer-aided composing. By means of this language the computer can do many things, for example, average between two melodic or rhythmic lines or gradually convert one rhythmic or melodic pattern into another. These averaging processes have produced pleasing results, particularly in view of the simplicity of the algorithm involved. Another possibility is combining functions of different periods to produce an overall function having a much longer period. Such a process frequently produces interesting sequences.

An example of the averaging process is shown in Exx. 7 through 10. In this example "The British Grenadiers" is gradually converted to "When Johnny Comes Marching Home" and back—a nauseating musical experience but one not without interest, particularly in the rhythmic conversions. The "Grenadiers" is written in 2/4 time in the key of F major. "Johnny" is written in 6/8 time in the key of E minor. The change from 2/4 to 6/8 time can be clearly appreciated yet would be quite difficult for a human musician to play. The modulation from the key of F major to E minor involving a change of two notes in the scale is jarring, and a smaller transition would undoubtedly have been a better choice.

Sixteen beats of "The British Grenadiers" (the latter half of the tune) are drawn in Ex. 7. As it is inconvenient and inaccurate to draw this number of beats across a single page, the frequency and duration functions have been, in effect, continued onto two pages. The drawing surface can be considered a cylinder with the right-hand side joined to the left-hand side. Functions can be continued simply by moving the pen back to the left-hand side and continuing drawing, as is shown clearly for the

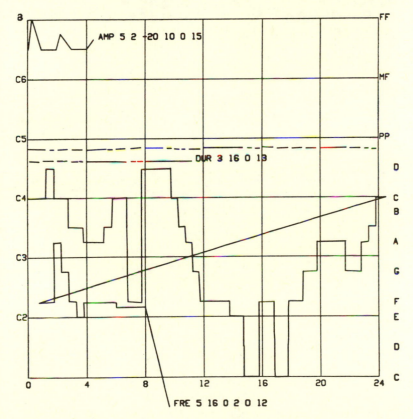

Ex. 7. Graphic Score for Grenadier-Johnny Transition

frequency function. The amplitude function produces both a primary and a secondary accent in each measure. Two units along the abscissa correspond to one beat. Thus the measures are indicated by the major abscissa divisions. The frequency function has been labeled 12, the duration function 13, and the amplitude function 15 for future reference in the algebra.

Example 8 shows the corresponding score for "Johnny." In this score it is convenient to make one beat of the 6/8 time equivalent to one abscissa unit. The entire 8-measure (48-beat) section takes 48 abscissa units to draw. The duration of this 8-measure section is 16 beats of the composition; thus one measure of "Johnny" will correspond exactly to one measure of the "Grenadiers." The duration line in "Johnny" happens to repeat exactly after four measures, so only four measures need be drawn. Again the amplitude function shows a primary and secondary accent. The amplitude, frequency, and duration functions are labeled respectively 17, 16, and 18.

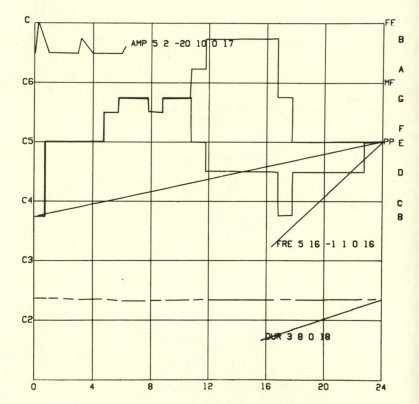

Ex. 8. Graphic Score for Grenadier-Johnny Transition (cont.)

The two averaging functions are shown in Ex. 9. In the algebra the frequency and duration function of the "Grenadiers" will be multiplied by function 20. Function 20 has a duration of 200 beats as compared with the 16-beat duration for one cycle of either melody. Its value is unity for the first 24 beats; it then decreases linearly to zero, is zero for 24 beats, and increases back to unity for the last 30 beats. The complementary function 21 starts at zero, builds up to unity in the middle, and decreases to zero at the end. The melodic line of the resulting composition will be formed as the sum of the melodic line of the "Grenadiers" multiplied by function 20 plus the melodic line of "Johnny" multiplied by function 21. Thus the melody will start with "The British Grenadiers," gradually be converted to "Johnny," and then be reconverted to the "Grenadiers."

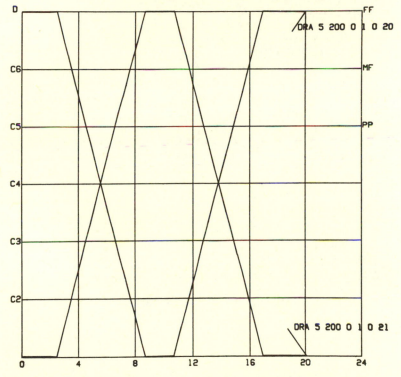

Ex. 9. Graphic Score for Grenadier-Johnny Transition (cont.)

One step in addition to averaging is required. The weighted average between simultaneous notes in "Grenadiers" and in "Johnny" would, in general, be a frequency not necessarily belonging to the scale of either "Grenadiers" or "Johnny." Hence the average is quantized against a scale which contains all the notes in either the scale of F major or E minor, that is C, D, E, F♯, G, A, B♭, and B.

The rhythmic functions are averaged in a manner similar to the frequency functions. The particular way in which the rhythm pattern is represented in the computer to allow such averaging will be discussed in detail in the next section. For the moment, we will simply state that the averaging process works like any other averaging.

The actual statements to the computer to perform the algebra are shown in Ex. 10. For convenience in programming these have been written in numerical parenthesis-free notation which uses binary operators placed as prefixes [9]. This notation is admittedly difficult to write and read, and in subsequent versions of the program it can be replaced by something more attractive.

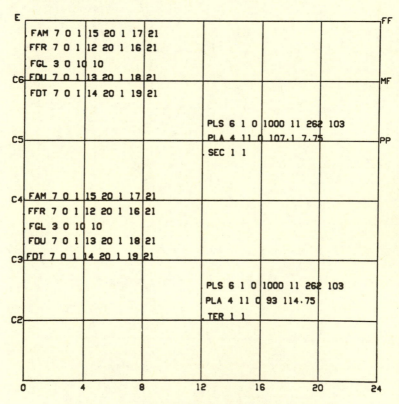

Ex. 10. Graphic Score for Grenadier-Johnny Transition (cont.)

Two operators are currently included, addition (represented by 0) and multiplication (represented by 1). Space is reserved in the program for other operators represented by the digits 2 through 9. Functions are represented by function numbers 10 through 89. Function 10 is a built-in function equal to zero, function 11 is a built-in function equal to unity.

As an example, the top line of Ex. 10 instructs the computer to form an amplitude function which in more conventional notation would be written

Amplitude Function $= [f_{15}(t) \times f_{20}(t)] + [f_{17}(t) \times f_{21}(t)]$

The functions 15, 17, 20, and 21 have already been defined in Exx. 7–9. An inspection of the notation will show that each binary operator is followed by two operands which may be either functions or the results of combining functions with operators.

The resulting notation affords a flexible and general way to construct complicated functions by combining simpler functions. It is basically a compositional tool or a language in which to express compositional ideas. In addition to averaging between two sequences, a second general use is combining functions with different periods, thereby constructing a function with a period much longer than any of its constituents. In this way a continually changing function which has certain inherent repetitive patterns can be produced; this class of functions produces an interesting compositional development.

Self-Synchronizing Functions for Durations

The representation of a melody by a continuous function of time which can be multiplied or added or otherwise operated on by an algebra is quite clear and straightforward. It is not so clear how this process can be extended so that an algebra can operate in any sensible fashion on note durations or a rhythm pattern. Although combining two rhythm functions by the logical operations of "and" or "or" is possible, these in general do not produce gradual changes in patterns. The two representations which will be described here represent the durational sequence as a continuous function of time which is amenable to averaging and which changes rhythm patterns in a manner which sounds reasonable. In other words, one pattern converts to another pattern by lengthening or shortening the notes which one might expect to change and by adding or subtracting notes at appropriate times if the two patterns have different numbers of notes.

Although a durational pattern is drawn as a sequence of dashes on the score, it is represented in the computer by a continuous function of time of the type shown in Ex. 11. Here a five-beat pattern is shown together with the conventional score for this pattern. The computer generates the rhythm pattern by operating on the stored function $f_1(t)$ with a standard algorithm. At the start of the pattern the algorithm reads the initial value of f_1, $f_1(0)$, and obtains the duration of the first note, which is 1.5 beats. It then generates a note 1.5 beats long and reads the value of f_1 at the beginning of the second note, $f_1(1.5)$. The value of the function is 0.5, the duration of the second note. The computer generates this note and then

QUARTER NOTE HAS ONE BEAT

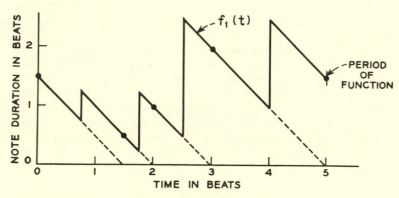

Ex. 11. Self-Synchronizing Function

reads function $f_1(2)$ to obtain the duration of the third note, etc. The function repeats at the end of five beats. Between the points marking the durations of the notes the function is made up of line segments having a slope -1 and discontinuities joining successive line segments. These discontinuities are arbitrarily located halfway between the starting points of successive notes. This rather peculiar shape of function was chosen because it makes the rhythm function invariant both to computational errors and to small changes introduced by the algebra. We shall refer to this form as a self-synchronizing function. For example, if the function is initially sampled not at zero but at some small time after zero, the slope of the function will produce a note just enough shorter than 1.5 beats so that the second note will occur at its normal starting time of 1.5 beats. In general, if a self-synchronizing function is entered at some point other than the starting time of one of the preplanned notes, one odd-length note will be produced and the subsequent sequence will be as planned. A number of experiments have shown that this self-synchronization property is very useful in maintaining the character of a rhythmic sequence in the face of the algorithmic changes made in a computer development.

The self-synchronizing function has a second pleasant property. If $f_1(t)$ and $f_2(t)$ are the self-synchronizing functions representing two different rhythmic sequences then any average $f_3(t)$ between these two,

$$f_3(t) = af_1(t) + (1 - a)f_2(t) \qquad 0 \le a \le 1$$

is also a self-synchronizing function. This property occurs because $f_1(t)$ and $f_2(t)$ are formed entirely of line segments with a slope of -1 and discontinuities, hence $f_3(t)$ must also be of the same nature. It is obvious that when a is 1, $f_3(t)$ equals $f_1(t)$ and when a is zero, $f_3(t)$ equals $f_2(t)$. Experimentally it has turned out that the development between rhythm pattern 1 and rhythm pattern 2 as a changes is both interesting and orderly for many rhythm patterns. This process allows the algebraic averaging which was described in the previous section to be applied to rhythm patterns. We find it a most useful compositional tool.

We have omitted one detail in the description of the rhythm function— the duty-factor function. The duration function specifies the time between the beginning of one note and the beginning of the subsequent note. The duty-factor function specifies the portion of time during which the note is actually playing, thus controlling the degree of legato or staccato in the style. In drawing the duration function, as for example function 13 in Ex. 7, the duty factor is inherent in the length of the dashes. The computer reads the length of the dashes and automatically constructs the duty-factor function and numbers it one higher than the duration function. In this example the duty-factor function would be 14. The function varies between 0 and 1, 0 corresponding to the ultimate and vanishing staccato, 1 to a slur. In playing simple tunes the duty-factor function is automatically supplied by the program. In more complicated algebraic developments it is usually desirable to average the duty-factor function in the same way the duration function is averaged. In Ex. 10 this is accomplished by the fifth statement from the top. Duty-factor functions 14 and 19 have been automatically constructed to go with duration functions 13 and 18, respectively; the algebraic statement combines these functions exactly as the duration functions have been combined.

One may ask, are there other representations for rhythmic sequences which have the same properties as the self-synchronizing functions which we have just described? An alternative computer rhythm function is shown in Ex. 12. Here the start of a note is represented by the positive-going zero crossing of a function and the termination of the note by the subsequent negative-going zero crossing. As shown, the function is made up of straight-line segments, but any function having a succession of zero crossings could be used. Two of these zero-crossing representations may be averaged in exactly the same way as the self-synchronizing functions are averaged; we have not tried this process, but it appears as though the average would have desirable psychoacoustic properties. The zero-crossing representation is even more general than the self-synchronizing function in that almost any algebraic operation on it will produce a legitimate rhythmic sequence, whereas allowable operations on self-synchronizing functions are basically limited to weighted averaging.

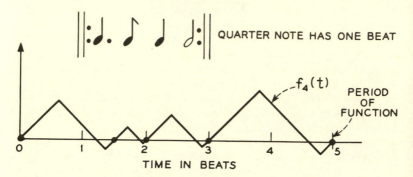

Ex. 12. Alternate Form of Self-Synchronizing Function

However, the zero-crossing representation would necessitate a searching process to find the zero crossings of the function when generating the rhythmic sequence; this process may be difficult and time-consuming on the computer.

Whichever process is used to represent durations, the overall result is the addition of a powerful development tool to the composer's arsenal of algorithms. The rhythmic averaging seems to be even more interesting than the frequency averaging and to make more psychoacoustic sense.

Metronome Markings

Metronome markings which give the relation between beats in the score and seconds of time in the sound have not been shown in any of the figures. They are treated exactly as has been described in the MUSIC IV Manual [5]. A numerical function made of straight-line segments is defined which specifies the tempo in terms of the standard metronome mark beats per minute. The tempo may change continuously with time to introduce accelerandos or ritards. For example, the statement

NUM 9   801   0   0   0   60   100   150   200   125

would specify at beat 0 a tempo of 60 beats per minute which is increased linearly to, at beat 100, a tempo of 150 beats per second which then decreases, at beat 200, to a tempo of 125 beats per second. In this case the tempo function consists of two straight-line segments, one specifying an accelerando, the other a ritard. As many segments as desired may be specified, thus approximating any given tempo as closely as is desired.

Pitch Quantizing

The PLS statement used in conjunction with frequency averaging requests a subroutine in the music program to quantize the frequencies of notes from the graphic functions. The pitch quantizing has been previously described [10]. The operation of the subroutine is to change the frequency of a note to equal the closest scale step of a pre-specified scale. In this way any small inaccuracies introduced in drawing the frequency function can be eliminated.

In the PLS statement in Ex. 4 the particular scale is described by numbers 262 (which gives the frequency of the fundamental of the scale in Hz) and 103 (which specifies the intervals in the scale). In this case, function 103 would contain the logarithmic intervals 0, 0.167, 0.333, 0.417, 0.583, 0.75, 0.833 corresponding respectively to C, D, E, F, G, A, and B♭.

It is also possible to use the pitch quantizing program to adjust the pitch of a note in a voice so that it forms one of a set of allowable intervals with the note in a second voice playing at the same time. In this way, it is possible to control the harmonic structure of the composition.

Conclusions

The experiments described in this article have three distinct implications. First, graphical input via a cathode-ray tube, light pen, and associated programs is an effective way for a man to communicate with a computer. Second, graphic scores are excellent ways of expressing many sound sequences. Third, the use of algorithms as an inherent part of the composition process is useful; or, in short, algorithmic composition is possible.

1. By means of the graphical-input computer, the composer is freed from the clerical drudgery of transcribing his scores into computer-readable form. Errors in the scores are immediately apparent and can be easily corrected by using the editing facilities of the graphical terminal. Hard-copy and machine-readable forms of the scores are produced. Finally, the use of a more-or-less real-time interaction system allows the composer to *hear* the sound sequence he has specified almost immediately, and make appropriate changes. Thus effective use is made of the best capabilities of both participants in the creative process—the machine supplying computational power, the human supplying judgment and direction as needed.

2. Graphic scores describe a sequence of sounds by three basic graphical functions; these specify the pitch, the note durations, and the loudness. The first two functions may be combined in a single line if desired.

Scores of electronic pieces serve two basic functions. They aid the composer in organizing and remembering his ideas; they aid the listener in following and learning the composition. Our experience leads us to believe graphic scores are substantially better than conventional scores for both these purposes. It is certainly easier to sketch and review ideas graphically. Details can be filled in or left out. The general development of passages can easily be seen. Melodies may be followed in general or in detail. In addition, we suspect the graphic scores will be easier to learn to read than conventional scores. The expression of pitch as position in the ordinate direction (free of the restrictions imposed by the music clef) and duration as a length in the abscissa direction (rather than an encoded "note" symbol) has direct intuitive validity.

It seems doubtful that graphic scores will replace conventional parts for instrumentalists playing a piece. However, the graphic language poses a generality for describing computer and electronic music which is completely beyond the capabilities of conventional scores. We expect a great deal of the music of the future will be scored graphically.

3. The basic tools for algorithmic composition which have proven effective are the periodic function, the algebra for combining these functions, the self-synchronizing function to represent durations, and the pitch quantizing subroutine. These devices are principally used to average between melodic and rhythmic patterns and to generate multiperiodic sequences in which functions with different periods are combined. A particularly effective combination consists of a melodic and a rhythmic line of slightly different periods.

By means of these algorithms many of the details of generating individual notes need not be completely written out. The composer can control the loudness, tempo, and number of voices by simple global functions which directly express his musical intentions. He can, with only slightly more work, control the degree of syncopation or synchronization between voices as well as the harmony and scale.

Is the computer composing? The question is best unasked but cannot be completely ignored. An answer is difficult to provide. The algorithms are deterministic, simple, and understandable. No complicated or not understood computations are involved; no "learning" programs are used; no random processes occur; the machine functions in a perfectly mechanical and straightforward manner. However, the result is sequences of sound which are unplanned in fine detail by the composer, even though the overall structure of the section is completely and precisely specified. Thus the composer is often surprised, and pleasantly surprised, at the details of the realization of his ideas. To this extent only is the computer composing. We call the process algorithmic composition. But we immediately emphasize again that the algorithms are transparently simple.

We believe algorithmic composition is the beginning of a revolution in the musical use of computers. The potentialities for composers of recorded pieces should already be clear. Additional possibilities will shortly arise when computers become fast enough, and cheap enough, for improvisation. The averaging functions for gradually modifying rhythmic and melodic sequences change slowly with time in a predetermined manner. These functions, rather than individual notes, can be under the direct control of the musician when improvising. He can linger near the averages which interest him and pass quickly through uninteresting combinations.

Finally, the compositional algorithms can be used to supplement technical knowledge, thus allowing music to be composed by people without formal training. If the day comes when each house has its own computer terminal, these techniques may make music as a means of self-expression accessible to everyone.

Appendix

Light Buttons and Operation Codes for Graphic Scores

INFORMATION is generated on the Graphic 1 by a set of 13 light buttons, a light pen, and a typewriter keyboard. We shall describe the operation of the light buttons.

FUNCTN: A tracking cross appears; the cross is moved with the light pen to the starting point of the function; button No. 1 is pressed to mark this point; the cross is moved to the next point on the function; button No. 1 is pressed again to mark this point, etc. Up to 100 points can be so designated. Straight-line segments, visible on the scope, connect the points. The function is completed by pushing a second button. A line of text must then be typed; it is terminated by typing a special escape character. The line can then be accepted, or deleted and retyped in case of error.

NOTES: Works the same as FUNCTN, except that the vectors drawn are alternately visible and invisible. This feature is used to draw a dashed line to specify times. The beginning of a dash specifies the beginning of a note; the end of the dash, the end of the note.

COPYALL: Asks the composer to select a music function or comment, which is then copied in its entirety. The copy must then be positioned via the tracking cross.

COPY FN: Works the same as COPY, except that if a music function is selected, the composer must type a new descriptor for the copy.

COMMENT: Allows the composer to type a comment which appears in the display, but is ignored by the display-analysis program in the 7094.

DELETE: Asks the composer to select a music function or comment to be deleted in its entirety.

RETYPE: Asks the composer to select the text to be deleted and retyped. If a music function is selected, its descriptor is deleted and must be retyped.

MOVE: Asks the composer to select a music function or comment to be moved via the tracking cross. A music function and its descriptor move together.

7094: Sets a signal for the 7094, which services the request on completing the job currently being processed. The waiting time varies from a few seconds to (typically) a few minutes.

LOAD: Allows the composer to load from the card reader a binary deck containing a score previously punched by the 7094 display-analysis program.

CLEAR: Clears the frame currently being displayed.

FRAME: Asks the composer to select the frame to be displayed and into which the succeeding new data are to be placed. A list of twelve frames lettered A to L is presented.

OVERLAY: Asks the composer to select the frame to be overlayed. The overlayed frame is displayed less brightly than the frame into which new data are being placed. Entities in the overlayed frame may be moved, copied, or deleted.

The form of information to the music program in the 7094 consists of a graphic function followed by a typed operation code and two or more numbers. A listing and description of these codes will be given next.

The operation code is a three-letter mnemonic which specifies the purpose of the function just drawn. The first number is a word count giving the number of numbers to follow. The rest of the numbers have various meanings for various operations. Numbers can be separated either by blank spaces or by a comma. The numbers can either contain or not contain decimal points.

In general only two numbers need be written after an operation code. Subsequent numbers, if not written, are given standard values by the program in some cases. These are called default values and are indicated in the description below.

Functions can be explicitly numbered from 12 through 49. If this is not done, the program will automatically number successive functions sequentially from 50 through 89.

Functions 10 and 11 are predefined as zero and unity respectively for all values of abscissa.

In the following list:

> W is word count
> P is period of function in beats
> B is value given the bottom line of grid
> T is value given the top line of grid
> F is function number

Default values are given in parentheses where used.

AMP—Draw amplitude function
AMP   W   P   B(−20)   T(10)   0   F

GLI—Draw glissando function
GLI   W   P   B(−3)   T(3)   0   F

FRE—Draw frequency function
FRE   W   P   B(−3)   T(3)   0   F

DUR—Draw duration function
DUR   W   P   0   F

Note: The program automatically constructs a duty-factor function to go with a DUR function and numbers it $F + 1$.

FAM—Compute amplitude function
FAM   W N_1 N_2 $N_3 \ldots N_w$

$N_i = 0$ stands for addition
$N_i = 1$ stands for multiplication
$10 \leq N_i < 89$ refers to functions by number
Example: The statement
FAM   9   1   0   1   12   13   0   14   15   16
is equivalent to
$(((f_{12} \times f_{13}) + (f_{14} + f_{14})) \times f_{16})$

FGL—Compute glissando function ⎫ Notation
FFR—Compute frequency function ⎪ is the
FDU—Compute duration function ⎬ same as
FDT—Compute duty-factor function ⎭ FAM

Note: The program *does not* automatically compute an FDT function, and a function corresponding to the FDU must be written out. See Ex. 10.
DRA—Draw a general function which can be used in an algebraic statement
DRA   W   P   B   T   0   F

PLA—Play a sequence of notes
Form 1: PLA   3   V   B   E
V instrument number
B beginning beat of sound
E ending beat of sound
All functions involved in the generation start at zero (abscissa) at beat B.

Form 2: PLA   4   V   B   E   P
V instrument number
B beginning beat of sound

E ending beat of sound
P initial value of all functions involved in the generation at beat B

DUF—Specify duration and frequency line together
DUF   W   P   B(−3)   T(3)   0   F

Note: DUF constructs three functions, a FRE, a DUR, and a DTY function and numbers them F, F + 1, and F + 2, respectively

SPT—Set parameter in third pass of MUSIC IV program
SPT   2   N   P

Parameter N is set to value P.

SPS—Set parameter in second pass of MUSIC IV
SPS   2   N   P

Parameter N is set to value P.

SPF—Set parameter in first pass of MUSIC IV
SPF   2   N   P

Parameter N is set to value P.

GEN—Generate a function in third pass of MUSIC IV
GEN   W P_1 P_2 P_3 ... P_{12}

This card works as any MUSIC IV parameter card with P_1 ... P_{12} being the parameters.

TER—Terminate composition
TER   1   1

PLS—Play a second-pass subroutine in MUSIC IV
PLS   W P_1 P_2 ... P_{12}

This card works exactly as any MUSIC IV parameter card with P_1 ... P_{12} being the parameters.

SEC—Terminate section
SEC   1   1

This card acts exactly as the SEC card in MUSIC IV.

CON—Continuation card
CON   W P_1 ... P_{12}

This card acts as an ETC card in MUSIC IV with P_1 ... P_{12} being the standard parameters.

NUM—Set parameters in numerical memory
NUM   W   X P_1 ... P_{12}

This card acts as a NUM card in MUSIC IV with P_1 ... P_{12} being the standard parameters and X the function number in which the parameters are stored. Note that if $1 \leq X \leq 800$, the parameters are stored in pass I. If X = 801, the metronome function is stored in pass II (see MUSIC IV handbook [5]) and if X > 801, parameters are stored in pass II.

References

1. David, E. E., Jr., Mathews, M. V., and McDonald, H. S., "A High-Speed Data Translator for Computer Simulation of Speech and Television Devices," Proc. Western Joint Computer Conf., March 1959.

2. Mathews, M. V., "An Acoustic Compiler for Music and Psychological Stimuli," *B.S.T.J.*, 40 (1961), pp. 677–94.

3. Mathews, M. V., "The Digital Computer as a Musical Instrument," *Science*, 142 (1963), pp. 553–57.

4. Pierce, J. R., Mathews, M. V., and Risset, J. C., "Further Experiments on the Use of the Computer in Connection with Music," *Gravesaner Blätter*, 27/28 (1965), pp. 92–97.

5. Mathews, M. V. and Miller, Joan E., "MUSIC IV Programmer's Manual," Bell Telephone Laboratories (unpublished).

6. Ninke, W. H., "GRAPHIC 1—A Remote Graphical Display Console System," Proc. Fall Joint Computer Conf., 27 (1965), p. 839.

7. Christensen, C., "GRIN (GRaphical INput) Language for the Graphic-1 Console," Bell Telephone Laboratories (unpublished).

8. Rosler, L., "The Graphic-1 7094 Graphical Interaction System and the GRIN94 Language," Bell Telephone Laboratories (unpublished).

9. Lukasiewicz, J., *Elements of Mathematical Logic* (Warsaw, 1929).

1 0. Mathews, M. V. and Miller, Joan E., "Pitch Quantizing for Computer Music," *JASA*, 38 (1965), p. 913(A).

1968

SOME MULTIPLE-SONORITIES FOR FLUTE, OBOE, CLARINET, AND BASSOON

JOHN C. HEISS

IN A previous article (on pages 114–16) I listed twenty-six multiple-stops (of two, three, and four tones) for the flute. As the result of recent investigations, I wish to present several additional such sonorities for flute, plus initial lists of similar sounds obtainable on the oboe, clarinet, and bassoon. I propose the use of the term "sonorities" in place of the term "stops," the latter term having specific meaning only in reference to stringed-instrument techniques.

While multiple-sonorities for woodwind instruments are more limited both in number and, for the present, ease of production than those played by stringed instruments, they are nonetheless a legitimate extension of the traditional performance capabilities of these instruments. They have not yet been widely used; however, their validity as compositional material is convincingly demonstrated in several recent works, such as those of William O. Smith on Contemporary Records #6010 and George Perle's *Three Inventions for Solo Bassoon*.[1] I have had some experience with their use in a work of my own entitled *Two Pieces for Three Flutes*.

The acoustic principle behind the production of the sonorities listed later in this article seems clear. In the majority of cases a fingering is employed which produces two or more possible tube-lengths for use in the production of tone. Several adjacent tone-holes on the upper portion of the instrument are closed while a single small hole, usually nearest to the embouchure and therefore *above* the closed holes, remains open. On the flute the small open hole is most often one of the trill holes; on the clarinet it is nearly always the hole opened by the octave key. (See illustration on p. 181.)

Similar methods of production are found on the oboe and bassoon, although with these instruments the technique of overblowing fundamental tones in the low register so as to obtain partials is also common.

Both the timbres of multiple-sonorities on woodwinds and the types of embouchure used in their production differ from the conventional norms. On the flute many of the sounds are relatively soft, not sharply focused, and, of necessity, short; the embouchure is rather "open" and the player should attempt a "spread" tone. For the clarinet the sounds are again generally soft, but they are all quite capable of being sustained – in fact they are the most successful this way, since their production often requires slightly more than

---

[1] Another group of fascinating sounds is presented in Donald Martino's Concerto for Woodwind Quintet. In this work the clarinetist obtains the tones of a harmonic series by closing all tone-holes and stopping the bell (which is pressed against the calf of the leg). Various additional pitches result from opening the octave or side keys.

For clarinet, the sonority listed as number 2 on p. 185.

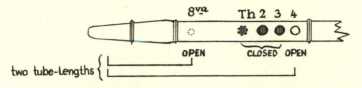

The shorter air column produces G
The longer air column produces E♭

(One might challenge the latter assertion by pointing out that this tube-length normally produces concert middle-C when the octave key is closed. Notice, however, that "left-hand 4" is the first large open hole on all double-sonorities having E♭ as the lowest note; notice that "left-hand 3" fulfills the same function when E♮ is the lowest note, etc.)

the usual attack time. The best embouchure combines normal placement of the mouthpiece with very loose pressure from the lower lip and teeth; the player must "aim" in between the two tones of a double-sonority, and into the middle region of the tones in triple- and quadruple-sonorities. The sonorities on the clarinet can only be given soft attacks.

The multiple-sonorities on oboe and bassoon, like those on the clarinet, are best when sustained. Their volume, however, ranges from medium to rather loud and penetrating, and the attack time is somewhat shorter. The embouchures are similar—generally a normal placement of the reed and very loose pressure from the lips, although an oboist may find somewhat greater success by inserting the reed just slightly more than usual. Bassoonists are advised to keep the throat rather closed and relaxed, as if about to pronounce a rolled, French "r."

Certain consistencies, in terms of interval, are apparent in the sonorities for the reed instruments. The double-sonorities for the clarinet are exclusively between tones on opposite sides of the register break; tenths and elevenths are the most frequent. The bassoon sonorities are mainly major 6/4 chords or combinations of partials resulting from a common fundamental. The fact that triple-sonorities predominate for oboe and bassoon is most likely due to the more complex vibrations of double reeds.

My notations are conventional. *Th, 2, 3, 4*, and *5* refer to fingers which are in their normal positions on each instrument unless otherwise specified. *Tr* stands for "trill-key." Black notes indicate short duration; white notes indicate tones which can be sustained. Small noteheads refer to softer tones

among a collection of louder ones. The designation 𝄐 means that a flutter-tongue timbre is associated with the production of the given pitches. (This is for the oboe and bassoon only. It is not the result of flutter-tonguing by the

player, and it seems to be unavoidable — though not necessarily undesirable —
in the specified cases.)

By way of conclusion, I wish to emphasize that I consider the following lists
as no more than an initial attempt at detailing what in time is likely to become
common material.[2] The multiple-sonorities are quite playable; they project,
and if practiced they may be performed with surprising facility.

I am indebted. to three students at the New England Conservatory —
Kenneth Roth, Ellen Polansky, and Yoshihide Kiryu — whose interest, imagination, and diligence account for much of the information presented
herein.

[2] That many additional such possibilities exist, perhaps for brass instruments also, is
demonstrated by the ease with which the following may be produced on the tuba:

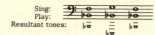

1968

	3b	15	15a	16	16a
Left Hand	Th, 2, 3, 4	Th, 2, 4	Th, 2, 3, 4
Right Hand	3 (tr), 4	4 (tr), 5 (Eb)	4 (tr), 5 (Eb)

	17	17a	17b	17c	18	18a	18b	18c
Left Hand	2, 3, 4	Th, 2, 4
Right Hand	5 (Eb)	2, 5 (Eb)

	19	19a	19b	19c	20
Left Hand	Th, 2, 3, 4, 5	Th, 2, 3, 4, 5
Right Hand	2, 3, 4, 5 (Eb)	2, 3 (open-hole), 4, 5 (Eb)

Ex. 1. Multiple-sonorities for Flute (to be added to those listed on pp. 115–16)

	1	2	3	3a	3b
Left Hand	2 (half-hole), 3, 4, 5 (B♭)	2, 3, 4, 5 (B)	2, 3, 4, 5 (B)		
Right Hand	2, 3, 4, 5 (C)	2, 3, 4, 5 (C)	2, 3, 5 (C)		

	4	5	6	7†	8†
Left Hand	2, 3, 4	2, 3, 4	2 (C♯ tr), 3, 4	2 (half-hole), 4	3, 4
Right Hand	2, 4, 5 (C)	3, 4, 5 (C♯)	2, 3	2, 3, 4 (F)	2, 3, 4 (F)

	9†	10†	11†	12	13†*	14†
Left Hand	3, 4	3, 4	3, 4	3, 4	3, 4, 5 (G♯)	2 (C♯ tr), 3, 4, 5 (G♯)
Right Hand	2		5 (C♯)	5 (E♭)	5 (C♯)	2

	15	16	17	18	19†
Left Hand	2 (C♯ tr), 3, 4, 5 (G♯)	2 (half-hole), 3	2 (half-hole), 3, 5 (B♭)	2 (half-hole), 4	2(half-hole),3,4,5(B)
Right Hand		3, 4, 5 (E♭)	2, 3, 5 (E♭)	2, 4 (F)	2 (G♯), 3, 4, 5 (E♭)

	20†	21	22	23
Left Hand	2 (half-hole), 3, 4	2 (half-hole), 3	2 (half-hole), 3	2 (half-hole), 4
Right Hand	3, 4, 5 (E♭)	2 (G♯), 3, 4, 5 (E♭)	2, 3, 5 (E♭)	2, 5 (C)

† These sound well and are easily produced.

* Try a slow trill between nos. 13 and 9.

Ex. 2.   Multiple-sonorities for Oboe

	1†	alternate fingering:	2		alternate fingering:
Left Hand	Th, 8ve key, 2, 3	Th, 8ve key, 2, 3, 4, 5 (C♯ key)	Th, 8ve, 2, 3		Th, 8ve, 2, 3
Right Hand	2, 3				2, 3, 4, 5 (F)

	3	4	5	6	7	alternate fingering:
Left Hand	Th, 8ve, 2, 3	Th, 8ve, 2, 3	Th, 8ve, 2, 3	Th, 8ve, 2	Th, 8ve, 2	Th,8ve,2,3,4(E♭)
Right Hand	2, 3, 4, 5 (F♯)	2, 3, 4	2,3,4,5 (G♯)	2, 3, 4, 5 (G♯)	2,(5 on G♯opt.)	

	7a	8	9	10	10a
Left Hand	Th, 8ve, 2	Th, 8ve, 2	Th, 8ve, 3, 4, 5 (C♯)	Th, 8ve, 3, 4, 5 (C♯)	
Right Hand	2, 3, 4, 5 (F)	2, 3, 4	2, 3, 5 (F♯)	2, 3, 5 (G♯)	

	11	12	alternate fingerings:		13	14	alternate fingering:
Left Hand	Th, 8ve, 3, 4, 5 (C♯)	Th, 8ve	Th, 8ve, 4	Th, 8ve, 2	Th, 8ve, 4	Th, 8ve	Th, 8ve, 4
Right Hand	opt. 3, 5 (E)	2, 3, 5 (G♯)	2, 3, 4, 5 (F)		2, 3, 4	2,3,4,5 (G♯)	2, 3

	15	16	17	18	19
Left Hand	Th, 8ve	Th,8vc,2,3,4	Th,8ve, 2,3,4,5 (C♯)	Th,8ve,2,3,4,5 (C♯)	Th, 8ve,2,3,4,5 (C♯)
Right Hand	5 (F♯)		2, 3, 4, 5 (E)	2, 3, 4, 5 (F)	2, 3, 4, 5 (F♯)

	20	20a	20b	21	22	23
Left Hand	Th, 8ve, 2, 3, 4, 5 (C♯)			Th, 8ve, 2, 3, 4	Th, 8ve, 2, 3, 4	Th, 2, 3, 4, 5 (C♯)
Right Hand	2, 3, 4, 5 (G♯)			3, 4, 5 (F)	3, 4, 5 (E)	2, 3, 4, 5 (E)

	24	25
Left Hand	Th, 2, 3, 4, 5 (C♯)	Th, 2, 3, 4, 5 (C♯)
Right Hand	2, 3, 4, 5 (F)	2, 3, 4, 5 (F♯)

†The double-sonorities in this list are more or less equal in quality. All are soft, clear, and easily produced.

Ex. 3.   Multiple-sonorities for B♭ Clarinet (notated at concert pitch)

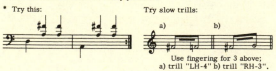

† These sound well and are easily produced.

* Try this:

Try slow trills:

a) b)

Use fingering for 3 above;
a) trill "LH-4" b) trill "RH-3".

‡ The best embochure for numbers 13-20 includes an open throat, the reed inserted more deeply than usual, and full pressure from the lips and lungs. (Here one is attempting to "overblow"; in numbers 1-12, one attempts to "underblow".)

Ex. 4.   Multiple-sonorities for Bassoon

NOTATION FOR PIANO*

ALOYS KONTARSKY

THERE has been so much valuable discussion of how contemporary music should be notated that I fear that, at this point, the
simplicity of my arguments will be found boring, if not actually
irritating. As a performer, I feel best qualified to approach the
question from the standpoint of performance practice. I am also
quite aware that there are those who are prepared to find the observations of a mere practitioner trivial. Notation which seems quite
feasible in the abstract, and looks extremely attractive on paper,
often turns out, once it is put into the hands of players, to be awkward, if not nonsensical, from a practical point of view. But a performer is suspect if he doubts the possibility of realizing some
delicate work of draftsmanship as music, or if he considers one of
the numerous nomenclature tables, which preface even minute and
harmless pieces, to be senseless, or if he even feels that some musical configuration would be easier to perform if it were written in
traditional notation. The suspicion aroused is that, among other
things, the player (he of little faith) regards the art of music the
way Aaron did the law of God. And incidentally, it was probably
no coincidence that Schoenberg had the character who dilutes
God's law sung by a tenor—tenors being generally considered real
scoundrels among performers.

Since a performer's function is to transmit material he did not
himself compose, there is great danger, no doubt, that he will dilute
or transform it by trying to make it conform to musical concep-
tions (notational or otherwise) with which he is already familiar.
This latent tendency toward appeasement manifests itself not only
in its crudest, and all too familiar, form: i. e., deference to what is
alleged to be the public taste; there are numerous examples of subtle bowdlerization in cases in which new music is seriously and
apparently uncompromisingly presented, which result from the fact
that the performer, consciously or unconsciously, has relied on
ideas from other music in preparing a new piece. I would like to
point out something which must be discussed more thoroughly at

*From *Notation Neuer Musik,* Vol. 9 of *Darmstädter Beiträge zur Neuen Musik,* 1964

a later point: performers often resort privately to standard musical symbols in the process of working out indeterminate or graphic scores. The beautiful picture created by the composer is marred by this practice, of course. If you have ever seen banal noteheads with stems, flags, and beams written into the score of a piece which was set up graphically, and then remembered the radical appearance of the symbols in the original score, then you know what I mean. Not infrequently, however, musicians have no choice but to use traditional notation when they are trying to realize a visual design in a way that is even somewhat adequate from a musical standpoint.

Let me give an example. In 1962, a young man came to my seminar in Darmstadt and played Earle Brown's *December '52*. He sat still in front of the score for a while, and then he improvised a rather disorganized muddle of single pitches, clusters, and figures. When I asked him how he had arrived at what seemed to me a senseless succession of events, he answered that he let the image of the page inspire him. I tried to suggest methods one might use to work out a performing score of the piece, such as drawing a staff to fix specific pitches, and I discussed various possibilities of temporal organization with him. But he rejected all my contrivances as sly tricks and insisted adamantly on his own inspiration. I do not wish to begin a polemic against irrationality in new music here (although one is long overdue), and I mention the current fatal affinity for mood-kitsch only in passing. I would much prefer to discuss my general approach to the problems presented by a score like Earle Brown's. I proceed on the assumption that what I find on the page is acceptable as a musical composition. The problem is to make an appropriate musical realization of a purely graphic pattern. In the case of Brown's piece, the page contains nothing but black lines and rectangular surfaces, all of which are either parallel or perpendicular to one another. I do not know whether the composer arrived at his arrangement by using some set of preferences, whether he left it to chance, or, conceivably, whether he produced it by using a statistical process. The visual impression, in any case, is rather ascetic: no curves, no coloring, no diagonals—simply straight lines and rectangular planes. Now, in order to produce an auditorially analogous result, it seems logical that I reduce my musical vocabulary equally drastically, to something like, for example, single pitches, clusters, and rests. So, to suggest the rectilinear appearance of the image to the listener, I worked out a version which,

I maintain, can be regarded as a musical translation of the graphic pattern of the score.[1]

I do not want to dwell on the issue of the intelligibility of graphic musical notation of this sort, since it is only one of the problems of contemporary notation. I want to report primarily on the numerous and varied performance directions with which we must work. Since the time that composers no longer felt obliged to use traditional notation, nearly every composer has developed his own private system of notation. The result is a huge number of symbols, a complete set of which must be learned just to prepare the performance of a single piece. The assertion, made occasionally, that the particular structure of a composition always requires its own method of notation seems very questionable to me, and, in any case, cannot justify the fuss. Time and again, two different symbols stand for a single action, or, conversely, a specific symbol has totally divergent meanings in two different pieces.

In what follows, I will discuss, in order, the symbols used in the past few years to designate pitch, duration, dynamics, and tone color. The material is naturally not complete, although I have tried to present as comprehensive a catalogue as possible. In addition to the new keyboard literature available to me, I have cited examples from Stockhausen's *Refrain* and his *Mikrophonie I* and have taken some symbols from the piano parts of compositions for chamber ensemble. I will not deal with contemporary scores written in traditional notation.

I. Pitch

The suspicion that traditional notation was no longer a sound means of representing new music was first aroused by the sheer number of accidentals in pieces. It was already a common problem by the late Romantic period, particularly because the attempt was still being made to relate chromaticism as closely as possible to the tonal framework. This led, of course, to a curious accumulation of double sharps and double flats, and correspondingly complicated

---

[1] The young man, by the way, argued completely in the spirit of the composer, which I did not know at the time, because we had only the particular page on hand and not the instructions for its use. They indicate, of course, as did the Darmstadt performance by a chamber ensemble, that the design was not to be interpreted as a model for a structurally analogous musical realization at all, but was intended, in fact, to stimulate the player(s) to make an improvisation, whatever its form. So the Darmstadt performance included trills, glissandi, crescendi, sforzati, and even all kinds of solo licks, which could not have been derived, with even the best of intentions, from the scanty design on the page.

resolutions, so that players often could not, so to speak, see the forest for the trees. In addition, the rules were unclear. Although an accidental was to be observed only within the measure in which it occurred, composers often put a natural sign in the following measure to avoid confusion. Similarly, one often encounters a natural sign on one staff, while on another staff an accidental appears which affects not the same pitch, but one in a different octave. The advance of chromaticism and the unfamiliar dissonances which arose from it induced composers to overnotate as a precaution against mistakes on the part of the players, who on the whole were not likely to be familiar with the latest developments. Reger produced classic examples of this kind of scarcely comprehensible notation, especially in very chromatic pieces like the *Introduction, Passacaglia, and Fugue for Two Pianos,* Op. 96. To my knowledge, the first attempt to arrive at a comprehensive system of notation stems from Busoni. He wrote, regarding his second Sonatina (1912): "The accidentals apply only to the notes before which they stand, so that natural signs are not used." This method has been widely used up to the present time. It is particularly appropriate for piano music in which there are wide leaps and disjunct progressions, but it is awkward and unpleasant to work with when one must play small intervals or melodic figurations. Years ago, for example, I had great difficulty learning Alois Haba's Toccata, Op. 38, not because it was pianistically or musically so difficult, but because the irregular scale passages it contains were notated by the Busoni method, and consequently were wretched to read. Stockhausen, who uses this method in his *Klavierstücke V-X,* has obviously considered this problem, because he occasionally helps the performer out by inserting natural signs to make reading easier.

Traditional notation has also survived up to the present. Boulez goes so far as to provide every note, on principle, with an accidental, with the result that the natural sign loses its original meaning, since it appears even when there is no accidental to cancel. Its sole function is to designate an unaltered note, which on the piano means the white keys.[2]

[2] I would like to mention a misleading notational practice which appeared in a piece for chamber ensemble (*Terms* by Peter Michael Braun). The composer placed all the accidentals over the notes, which is foolish for chords which are to be played on the piano, inasmuch as the pianist must read each chord twice, once for the pitches themselves, and once for the accidentals. In addition, he must guess which accidental belongs to which pitch. This is an example of the kind of arbitrary innovation which arises constantly.

In 1957, Henri Pousseur developed a new method, in *Mobile* for two pianos. Instead of using accidentals, he designs the notehead itself to indicate the exact pitch to be designated: a black notehead indicates "no accidental" and a white notehead indicates "flat."

Needless to say, this method will work only if the whiteness or blackness of noteheads ceases to have temporal meaning. If a composer wants to use this method, he must find another way to notate duration. Pousseur's method is easy for pianists to read, and works so long as no enharmonic notes creep in: "F flat" and "C flat" are meaningless, because they contradict the practical correspondence between the color of the notehead and the color of the key.

Interestingly enough, Mauricio Kagel developed the same principle at almost the same time, in *Transicion* for piano, percussion, and tape; but he has the white notehead indicate the "natural" pitch and the black notehead the "sharped" pitch:

When I asked Kagel why he had decided to reverse Pousseur's practice, he answered that he thought his own method psychologically better, because the white notehead corresponds to a white key and the black notehead to a black key. Although this argument seems valid, I still have difficulty reading Kagel's scores, whereas I can sight read many-voiced chords from a score written in Pousseur's notation. Why should this be so? I think the reason is that pianists unconsciously regard white keys as the norm and black keys as the exception. Every pianist began with the white keys and learned to use the black keys only at a later point; there are also more white keys than black keys. The same thing is true of black and white noteheads when they are regarded as durational symbols. The black notehead is generally considered the norm under those circumstances, perhaps because there are so many more forms of black notes (quarter, eighth, sixteenth, thirty-second, etc.) than white notes (half note and whole note). Thus, one might prefer

Pousseur's method for psychological reasons, or Kagel's because of the visual appearance of the score.[3]

Another problem in the notation of pitch arises because composers—especially since the beginning of serial composition—love wide leaps. Frequent use of the extreme registers makes the use of numerous ledger lines necessary, and they are difficult to read when the pitches involved are among the highest or lowest on the piano. Since ledger lines are not grouped, pianists have to look very closely to distinguish the number of lines. The normal octave sign *8ve - - - -*, or even the two octave sign *15ve - - - -*, are not always helpful either. Even though ledger lines are often unintelligible, they nonetheless give a clear picture of the distance between pitches and enable one to gauge immediately how far to move one's hand; but the octave signs tend to conceal the size of a leap and can even fool players into moving in the opposite direction.

I first encountered an attempt to combine the advantages of both possibilities in a composition for two pianos by Ernst Albrecht Stiebler called *Klangmomente* (1961). Stiebler uses four systems, the inner two of which correspond to the customary systems, and the outer two of which indicate, at any given time, a transposition of two octaves, either up or down.

This notational method makes it possible to identify the pitch in question immediately. And what is more, the different lengths of

---

[3]The author hereby requests all interested readers not to try the two other alternatives when using this method of notation:

Since Pousseur's notation is easy to read, composers should refrain from devising additional variations, especially because it may safely be assumed that Pousseur considered the other possibilities himself. There is no point in discovering the North Pole a second time.

note stem which result from the spatial distance between the systems correspond graphically to changes in pitch level and to changes in the direction in which a player must move his hand.[4]

The notation for trills and clusters should be mentioned in conjunction with the notation of pitch. The trill sign has not been altered up to the present time, and it is not surprising, because it is the classic example of a successful symbol: it gives a clear picture of what is to be played. Its only disadvantage is that it, properly speaking, is connected to a reference pitch which the player consciously or unconsciously favors, but this disadvantage seems minimal when one considers that the trill symbol designates both the pitches *and* the duration of the trill equally well.[5]

We now need to consider how best to notate the second pitch of the trill. The old method of putting an accidental either above or below the wavy line is not really clear:

It will work only so long as it is possible to guess from the context which pitch is intended. The following method is always unambiguous, particularly because it can represent a trill whose span exceeds that of a major second:

There has always been a clear symbol for the trill,[6] but that is not the case for clusters.

---

[4]Incidentally, there is already a variant on this method of notation: Helmut Lachenmann notates his *Echo andante* (Munich, 1962) in the same fashion, using four systems, but he transposes the outer systems up or down just one octave.

[5]Originally, the trill was an embellishment, a reinforcement of a given pitch, and not a rapid alternation of two pitches. For that there is the symbol:

which, of course, is not so graphically compelling a visual image as the standard trill symbol.

[6]No symbol is so clear, however, that some composer won't be tempted to devise something else: thus, Hermann Josef Kaiser (in *Pas de deux pour deux pianos,* 1963) created several new trill symbols which I urgently implore composers not to adopt. Here an almost perfect symbol, which is intelligible in every instance, is capriciously replaced by four other symbols which, moreover, are very difficult to distinguish from one another.

I will not dwell on the various methods of attack for clusters here, since Kagel has discussed them in his well-known article "Toncluster, Anschläge, Übergänge" (*Die Reihe,* Vol. 5, p. 23), but will consider only the composition of the cluster, that is, whether it is to be executed on the white keys, on the black keys, or on both. If a composer writes clusters for a keyboard instrument which are principally chromatic, the notation is unproblematic; but if he wishes to take the particular location of the keys into account, then the notation can be confusing. Ives and Cowell, who wrote the first clusters, notated them as a kind of chord, a combination, so to speak, of a C major triad and an F♯ major triad. It seems fussy, but it is impossible to misinterpret.[7]

Today there are numerous symbols for clusters, even though the playing technique is rather simple. For clusters on the white keys:

For clusters on the black keys:

These same symbols, however, can designate clusters of both black and white keys. There is, in addition, a whole set of symbols which I will not discuss here.

The pianist who must orient himself to these symbols is like the driver for whom a red light means "stop" in Darmstadt, and "go" in Donauschingen; but in Palermo he can choose between the two possibilities, or he can even decide to do something else altogether, like getting out of the car and continuing on foot.

II. Duration

The classical notation of durations was adequate for a relatively long time. Frequent changes of meter, which were made famous by *Le Sacre* and are characteristic of many scores from the 1920's, created the first difficulties. They signaled the approaching demise of traditional phrase lengths, but the meters themselves were still based on a common denominator. *Les Noces* is a good example of

---

[7]See Charles Ives, Second Pianoforte Sonata (second edition), p. 25, and Henry Cowell, *Exultation* and *Tiger*, both in Henry Cowell, *Piano Music,* New York, 1960 (AMP).

this: the reiterative schemes are repeatedly interrupted, but they never destroy the continuous eighth-note pulse. (The metronomic change at rehearsal number 9 only appears to deviate from this principle: the relationship is now 3:2, three-eighths of the new 2/4 measures corresponding to one-quarter of the preceding measure.) All of this could be notated by traditional methods. So long as there continued to be a smallest common note value, there was no fundamentally new problem of notation.

The old notation became impractical when duration was freed from common meter. New proportions came into play, above all those which had previously been regarded as "irrational rhythms": triplets, quintuplets, septets, and more complicated divisions.[8]

Composers first tried to adapt new structures to the familiar metric divisions. Boulez, for instance, added a supplement to his Flute Sonatina which rendered the *physionomie réelle* of mm. 296-339. In the score, the passage is compressed into a metrical scheme, which has nothing to do with the musical structure and serves merely to facilitate the synchronization of the two players. Stockhausen's *Kontrapunkte* offers a still better example, with its 3/8 measures da capo al fine. The conductor steadfastly beats time, while the music one hears bears no relation to his gestures. The bar lines are nothing more than an attempt to coordinate the players and could just as easily have been drawn elsewhere in the score, since there is no evidence that the meter has any musical significance whatsoever.

It became clear with the first *Klavierstück* of Stockhausen that the metrical proportions had become too complicated to be notated in the customary manner. A glance at the first measure shows that the available notation no longer suffices. There is probably no one capable of playing the first measure as written, namely, by subdividing 5/4 into 11 and later into 13 equal parts.[9]

---

[8]It was these irrational rhythms which stimulated Henry Cowell to make his first attempt to change our notational system radically. In his piano piece *Fabric* (contained in Henry Cowell, *Piano Music,* New York, 1960) he recommends that the different proportions be represented by different kinds of notehead:

$\text{♩} = 1/4 \quad \text{♩} = 1/6 \quad \text{♩} = 1/5 \quad \text{♩} = 1/7 \quad \text{♩} = 1/9 \quad \text{♩} = 1/11 \quad \text{♩} = 1/13 \quad \text{♩} = 1/15$

It hasn't proved workable. The symbols are too much alike, which is a criticism it seems we must often make of newly invented notations. In this case, the piece itself is really too simple to justify such a drastic change in notation; and this extravagance itself points to the foibles of a later generation of composers.

[9]In a later edition of *Klavierstücke I-IV,* Stockhausen himself recommends that the complicated fractions be converted into metronomic values.

Composers have had to search for other possibilities, and two divergent tendencies have emerged: the first is to try to preserve traditional notation in whatever ways are meaningful, and to make it more flexible by devising various tricks; the second is to depart completely from the traditional notation of duration in favor of a purely spatial notation. The second method was developed by the American School. Space notation has by no means become a standarized notational practice, but one can group together several distinct notational methods under this heading. The simplest of these is time-notation, so-called, which is the speciality of Cage and Brown. Stockhausen has written about time-notation in his excellent article "How Time Passes." In it he points out, among other things, that time-notation does not produce greater precision on the part of players; instead, precisely those details composers expected to get from using the notation are leveled out by the visual guesswork involved in reading it.

The following, from Stockhausen's *Refrain,* is an example of free notation of duration:

The second event follows when the held G dies away. In this case, the duration is dependent on the intensity of the sound, which is clearly illustrated by the tapering stroke.

In Stockhausen's *Mikrophonie I* it is relatively easy to perceive the spatial relations of the black dots:

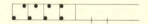

And they can be played in a way that corresponds rhythmically to their spatial relations:

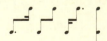

A performance from the graphic notation is likely to be somewhat less exact than a performance of the same passage notated in eighth notes; but even in graphic notation, the whole shape will be perceptible.

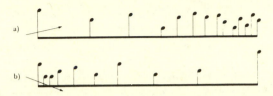

This example is also easy to read. The spaces between the individual notes clearly indicate a) an accelerando and b) a ritardando. This simple and practical method of notating duration is used frequently. Its use becomes crucial as soon as complicated time values are introduced.

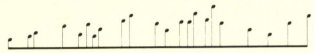

An experienced player could certainly read this figure effortlessly, but it could easily become incoherent in performance if the player failed to make the rhythmic relationships correspond exactly to the distances between the individual notes. On the whole, one can say that space notation is a useful way to notate passages in which little differentiation of note values is intended, because the player can perceive the whole progression quickly. This kind of notation is also recommended if the composer intends a certain degree of indeterminacy. For precise and detailed notation, on the other hand, traditional notation is probably preferable.[10]

The next few examples contain what seem to me to be very skillful attempts to adapt classical notation to new requirements. In this example, the composer enlists the aid of the metronome:

[10]The composer should relegate the working out of the microstructure of a piece to the performer only if he wants to grant him real freedom of decision. Translating graphic patterns into exact notation is not the job of an instrumentalist.

Whenever appropriate, Boulez puts metronomic values above the system and indicates accelerandi and ritardandi by using arrows which point up or down. In *Klavierstück VI* Stockhausen even adds an additional system to the score, each line of which signifies a kind of scale of metronomic values, which are indicated on a continuous line. Kagel uses the same method in *Transicion II*.[11]

Grace notes offer an additional possibility for releasing classical duration from its dependence on a metric pulse. Stockhausen lets the notes in small print fall outside the meter; thus the meter can be freely interrupted, in each case the degree of interruption depending on the ability of the player.

Boulez likes to use grace notes to blur the meter:

The arrows indicate whether the grace notes are to fall on the beat or before it. It is played something like this:

Here, in contrast to the Stockhausen example, the overall duration of the phrase is not altered. In both cases, however, the larger the grace-note group, the more serious the distortion of the meter. Of course, one could also make such interpolations independent of the established tempo by treating them as accelerandi and ritardandi. This method, combined with the use of the metronomic scale

[11]See Stockhausen, *Texte zur elektronischen und instrumentalen Musik,* Vol. 1, p. 238. This method presupposes, of course, that the player has developed something like a sense of absolute tempo. Unfortunately, this skill—in contrast to that of absolute pitch— is not part of the training given by music schools. Apparently, the metronome (not to mention the stopwatch) has an unmusical smell about it.

mentioned above, enables one to articulate differentiated durations rather precisely.

The score of Kagel's *Transicion II* is a successful blend of traditional and free notation of duration. He uses four systems, the lower two of which are notated normally and are compulsory, and the upper two of which are in free durations and may be added at the discretion of the player.

A short note on rests: in pure space notation, they are left out altogether, unless the composer needs symbols to articulate the microstructure of the piece:

Classical notation, of course, uses the familiar symbols:

Although the two methods are sometimes combined, as mentioned, new proposals have been made for the notation of rests. Breath marks are often combined with fermatas and then scaled. In Stockhausen's *Refrain,* the durations of the rests are precisely quantified:

$$\smallint = 0{,}5"   \vee = 1{,}0"   \wedge = 1{,}5"   \frown = 2{,}5"   \sqcap = 4{,}0"$$

Graphically, the series of symbols is well chosen, because as you move through the series, the symbols get larger as the durations increase. Boulez, unfortunately, prefers a different arrangement in which the rests are without specified durations: ⅄ ⊓ ⊓̄ ⌒ ⌒̄, which means that two divergent notational methods are being practiced.[12]

In reality, there are many more symbols in use because, unfortunately, many young composers fail to find out what their "established" colleagues have used successfully; instead, they come up with solutions to notational problems which they claim to have invented "completely on their own," solutions which players must learn just to perform a single piece. I will admit, however, that the symbols scarcely differ from one another: it is simply that their meaning changes from time to time.

[12]Kagel has noted that Boulez's series represents a departure from the French tradition, in which ⌒ ⌒̄ comes before ⊓ ⊓̄ .

III. Dynamics

Whereas pitch and duration can be fixed exactly, the notation of intensity, or dynamic level, is indeterminate. Only electronic music makes the exact specification of amplitude possible; in live instrumental music, the realization of notation for dynamics remains both relative and idiosyncratic. The situation is no different for contemporary music than it was for older music, and on the whole, the old symbols have not been replaced with new ones. Bo Nilsson suggested a new system in his *Quantitäten* for piano (1958) whereby intensities are scaled from 1.0 to 10.5, but it was not successful because the numbers simulate a degree of precision which no instrumentalist can ever attain. The concepts "forte" and "piano" are relative, and what is more, their interpretation by a performer is inevitably affected by his technique, the quality of the instrument, the size of the room, etc.

Ives made an interesting attempt to modify the meaning of the familiar symbols in the fourth movement of the *Concord Sonata*. He uses the customary symbols, from pppp to ff, but requests that the whole movement be played at a reduced dynamic level.[13]

Occasionally, there are similar performance directions in new pieces. In Stockhausen's *Mikrophonie I,* framed dynamic markings $\boxed{f}$ $\boxed{p}$ indicate the basic dynamic level of a group, which then contains further more detailed dynamic indications. Here and there one finds an attempt to designate different intensities by using different sizes of notehead. The effect is similar to that of space notation: at first glance, one can easily take in the large-scale changes in dynamic level; but at a more detailed level, the notation cannot be realized with the same precision one can attain using the customary symbols.

IV. Tone Color

Those aspects of sound produced on a piano which are usually identified as its "timbre" are created by using two different techniques: the first, which provides normal piano playing with shading, involves distinctions brought about by using different kinds of touch and the various pedals; the second has to do with playing inside the piano, either on the strings or on the case. The notational

---

[13]"This movement is supposed to be played in a lower dynamic ratio than usual, i. e., the 'f' here is about the 'mf' of the preceding movements."

problems involved are correspondingly different. We will begin with conventional piano playing.

The development of differentiated modes of attack has always been an individual problem, and these kinds of attack themselves continue to elude more exact description. The symbols composers use to suggest particular kinds of touch to players are by no means standardized, and, in any case, a uniform notation has never existed. I am reminded, for example of the wedge (∕) which Mozart used and which normally signifies a strong accent, a kind of staccato-sforzato, but which Mozart in all likelihood intended as a stress, and not as a staccato. Such examples abound. The meaning of these symbols has changed over time—and even within the works of a single composer—and their interpretation ultimately resides with performers. Needless to say, there are as many varieties of performer as there are schools of playing. Backhaus's staccato is different from Rubenstein's and Rubenstein's is unlike Kempff's. A pianist's quality and individuality are functions of the particular kind of sound he is capable of producing.

The indeterminacy of symbols for touch is also a result of the fact that touch cannot be treated as a separate problem: it is dependent on dynamics, on rhythmic articulation, and even on pitch to a certain extent, because the quality of the sound of a modern piano changes with the pitch level: a staccato in the bass sounds different from a staccato in the treble. These factors make even the current symbols ambiguous. . ⌐ ∪ ∕ ∧ ♦ indicate only approximately how the pitches they accompany are to be played.[14]

Kagel tried to achieve an exact definition of touch—although only for clusters—by specifying the height of the attack (in centimeters from the keyboard) and the speed of the attack (in metronomic values). It turns out, however, that these indications have more effect on a player's gestures than they do on the sound he produces, and consequently, the playing appears weirdly stiff and ceremonial—an effect which is probably intentional.

It *is* possible to give exact directions for the use of the pedals, but it requires an intimate knowledge of piano playing. Even composers who possess this kind of familiarity should consider very

---

[14]Symbols designating different kinds of attack are often intended as accents which affect the dynamics and the rhythm of a passage and are not meant to convey touch primarily. The Piano Suite, Op. 25, by Schoenberg is an example of this, in which ∕ and ∪ are used to disrupt the normal succession of strong and weak beats within a measure. ∕ means played as a strong beat and ∪ means played as a weak beat.

carefully whether detailed pedal indications are necessary. I might
mention in this connection that Debussy himself—the pedal composer par excellence—almost completely eschewed instructions for
the use of the pedal (unless one regards slurs, which indicate *laissez
vibre,* as such). Wanting to notate the pedal, especially the right
pedal, accurately enough to match the performance of an experienced pianist is asking too much. Let me give an example of why
this is so. When the pedal indication is placed beneath the note to
be affected, for instance, it does not mean literally that the key and
the pedal are to be depressed at the same time: this is done only
when a special echoing sound is desired. But if a composer should
try to specify the exact amount of time which should elapse between the depression of the key and the depression of the pedal,
he will discover that it depends on the kind of instrument being
used, whether the pitch being stated is in the treble or in the bass,
and whether the pitch is loud or soft. To include specifications of
this sort in the notation will only succeed in confusing players.
Wise composers restricted their use of pedal signs to places in which
a group of pitches "unter Wasser stehen soll," as pianists' jargon
would, appropriately enough, have it.

The displacement of the hammers caused by the depression of
the soft pedal has an effect not unlike a change in register, and use
of the soft pedal is, on the whole, less closely connected to the
subtle details of playing than is use of the right pedal. On most
pianos, the reduction in volume is accompanied by a hollow, musty,
nasal sound, because the well-worn part of the hammer does not hit
the string. The notation for the soft pedal itself is unproblematic.

In most cases, there is no need for a notational symbol for the
third (the sostenuto) pedal because it can be indicated by name in
the score. Unfortunately, however, not all composers understand
the mechanics of the third pedal. A direction like this one:

P⎯⎯⎯⎯⎯⎯⎯⎯⎯⏋
   3. P⎯⎯⎯⎯⎯⎯⎯⎯⏌

is completely wrong, because the third pedal can have no further
effect once the dampers have been raised by the right pedal. The
correct notation is simply:

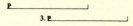

The following is also meaningless:

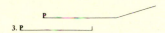

A gradual release of the pedal has no effect at all, since the third pedal influences the damping only indirectly. To obtain the desired result, the player must either release the key(s) gradually, or must utilize the right pedal in the following way:

The next example is feasible only if the player has the other hand free to depress the designated key during the pizzicato. The third pedal prolongs the damping already in progress but does not itself raise the dampers.

Finally, one should never notate the sostenuto pedal like this:

because the pedal works only after the key has been depressed, i. e., after the dampers have already been lifted.

If a composer insists on using all three pedals, I recommend the following method:

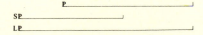

(SP seems to me to be a good abbreviation for sustaining pedal—the third pedal, developed by Steinway—or for the Italian term, *sostenuto pedal.*) The three pedals should be written under one another in the score in the order that they are mounted on the piano. As on the keyboard, one reads top to bottom as right to left. The indication for the third pedal should never be placed *under* that for the left pedal. This arrangement, which is not a good one, continues to be used because the sostenuto pedal is still considered somewhat exotic, perhaps because it was added last to the piano. The ordering—right pedal, left pedal, sostenuto pedal—is disconcerting for players. It uses customary terminology (third pedal), but the footwork involved is not taken into account.

The continuous line in the example below conveys finer distinctions in foot pressure than can be indicated by the old pedal notation.

If composers want to make minimal use of the pedal and leave the rest up to performers, they should use the conventional symbols and not invent new ones.[15]

The sounds obtained through manipulation of the strings or the case of the piano first played a role in music after the Second World War.[16] There is no tradition of notation for these sounds and consequently there is no comparable confusion anywhere in music. It is really astonishing, especially because the confusion surrounds what amounts to completely concrete playing directions, which in no way involve the kinds of ambiguity which complicate the specification of dynamics and timbre. The literature is an adventure if for

---

[15]The symbols used by B. A. Zimmermann in *Perspektiven,* for example, are unclear because they are too much alike:

                ∟ = depress the right pedal

                Γ = raise the right pedal

                ⌐ = depress the left pedal

                ⌐ = raise the left pedal

It is easy to confuse these symbols, especially when they follow one another closely.

Another of Zimmermann's attempts is interesting: in *Konfiguration,* the pedal durations are given in note values. It is easy to read, but, despite its precise appearance, it designates the sensitive right pedal too inexactly. Players are used to executing duration symbols at the moment at which they occur, and this does not correspond to standard pedal technique. (See Zimmermann, *Perspektiven* for two pianos, 1955-56, Schott, and *Konfiguration,* 1956, Schott.)

---

[16]Two remarkably early examples occur in Henry Cowell's piano pieces *Aeolian Harp* (1923) and *The Banshee* (1925).

no other reason than the sheer capriciousness of the notation. I have found the following symbols to designate a simple pizzicato (and there are certainly more):

And for another technique, damping the vibrating strings with the hand or finger:

The first five symbols of both groups are identical, but the others are completely arbitrary and are anything but unambiguous. The only notes in the examples which are not misleading are those labeled "pizz." or "mute." On the other hand, even the abbreviation "P" for pizzicato is risky, because most pianists will spontaneously read it as "piano."

In the following list of symbols, notice how the confusion is magnified by abbreviations from different languages: "F" suddenly no longer means "forte," but "finger," while in another piece, the Italian *dito* or abbreviated, "d," is used for "Finger"; "m" can mean "mute," or the previously noted damping of the string(s) with the finger or hand, but it can also come from the Italian *mano* and indicate that the hand is to strike the strings. To indicate normal playing on the keys, I have found the following abbreviations, among others: T = taste, k = keys, n = normal, ord. = ordinario. I leave it to the reader to make his way through the following list of symbols. This is only a *small* selection.

d = finger

D = damper

♪ = fingernail

d = fingertip

Fk = fingertip

Fn = fingernail

Fs = felt mallet

T = triangle beater

T = damp the strings at the bridge

T = lay triangle on the strings

A detailed discussion of the soundness of these different methods of notation is not possible here. Basically, the problems created by this group of symbols are trivial in comparison to the problems associated with the notation of duration, which depends in a crucial way on compositional structure. The symbol one chooses to represent pizzicato has no musical relevance; once a convention has been established, it can be applied to all kinds of music. This is an area in which composers, instrumentalists, musicologists, and publishers can work out joint recommendations without arousing the suspicion that they are operating in collusion to influence the course of music itself.

—Translated by Vernon Martin
(with the assistance of Jane Coppock)

1972

THE FLUTE: NEW SOUNDS

JOHN C. HEISS

IN TWO previous articles (on pages 114–16 and 180–86) I reported on the possibilities of playing multiple-sonorities on woodwind instruments, and gave lists for flute, oboe, clarinet, and bassoon of those sounds I consider most dependable. Recent developments in the sound-production possibilities on my own instrument, the flute, lead me to offer an updated report. Several of the techniques introduced here are, to the best of my knowldge, my own dis-coveries; others have become known to me through contact with other com-posers and performers. My information, however acquired, is naturally limited. The whole subject area of new performance techniques is quite vast and still growing,[1] even just for the flute. Many performers and composers currently have their own individual techniques and fingering charts for new sounds.[2] The present need appears to be one of communication and consolidation, and it is in this spirit that I offer what follows.

The techniques presented here are divisible into four categories: (I) exten-sion of the low register of the flute, with modified timbre, by an octave downward, (II) production of "harmonics," or more precisely, muted tones in the conventional low register, (III) introduction of noise elements into normal tone, and (IV) recently discovered multiple-sonorities.[3]

I. Extended Low Register

One of the modified timbres associated with the extension of the low register is the familiar and, indeed, now venerated key-slap, the earliest instance of which occurs in Varèse's *Density 21.5* (1936). Flutists generally agree that the best method of production for key-slaps is to finger the de-sired note, then raise and slap closed the G-key with the fourth finger of the left hand. This produces the maximum possible volume—a necessity since the sound, although quite percussive, is rather soft in the absence of any air blown through the embouchure. The effective range for key-slaps without air

[1] Even so seemingly comprehensive a book as *New Sounds for Woodwind (sic)* by Bruno Bartolozzi (Oxford University Press, 1967) is, as the author points out, no more than an introduction to the subject. There are no duplications whatsoever, for example, between Bartolozzi's lists and the information offered herein.

[2] Several prominent flutists who come to mind are Robert Cantrick, David Gilbert, Patrick Pursewell, and Harvey and Sophie Sollberger.

[3] Since precise verbal description of the timbres produced with the above techniques is difficult, if not impossible, composers are advised to consult with performers.

is thus low B up a minor sixth to the aforesaid G.[4] To obtain key-slaps with-out air in the next lower octave *one simply changes the instrument into a closed pipe.* This may be accomplished by carefully and completely covering the blowhole with the curve on the lower lip between mouth and chin. Clearly articulated pitches then result through use of the normal G-key slapping technique. Interestingly, however, these pitches are much closer to the *major seventh* below the fingered pitch than to the octave below it. (This is

*The actual pitch sounds a major seventh lower than the notated pitch.

Ex. 1. From Heiss, *Movements for Three Flutes*

[4] The instructions "without air" and "with air" are becoming common, which is to the good since there is a clear difference. "With air" actually means, "Use a little bit of air to gain resonance, but allow the primary sound to be that of the slap." Notations vary.

I propose 𝄽 for "without air," 𝄽 for "with air," and also 𝅝 for a sustained tone which is to be attacked sharply through the assistance of a key-slap. This latter effect is pos-sible throughout the entire range of the instrument, either directly or by simulation with the tongue for pitches above G in the low and middle registers. (Simulation with the tongue also works well for key-slaps *"with air"* above G.) The first two of the above notations call for sounds which must naturally be of short duration.

readily understood if one compares the closed pipe key-slap to the open pipe slap without *any* embouchure contact between instrument and player. In this case, the difference interval is more nearly an octave.)

One may obtain the pitches above the fingered G (sounding A♭ below low C) by slapping the lowest available key with the right hand index finger. Although the sounds produced in this way are of somewhat less intensity than the others, they are useful nonetheless. (Key-slaps "without air" above G in the conventional low register are considerably softer than their counterparts a major seventh below, and for this reason are less useful.) A suggested notation is that shown in Ex. 1, a passage from my *Movements for Three Flutes* (1969) in which these sounds project well.

A second timbre for the projection of sounds below the traditional range involves pressing both lips into the blowhole and playing with a trumpet-like embouchure, making the lips vibrate. The flutist Patrick Pursewell has a reputation for considerable proficiency with this technique, which is used in a piece of his entitled *It Grew and Grew*.

II. Low Register "Harmonics"

It is normally assumed that harmonics on the flute begin at the first available point for overblowing a fundamental, namely one octave above low B. Non-conventional fingerings may be used, however, to produce tones of various timbres below this pitch down to low D♯.[5] Example 2 gives fingerings which produce muted, soft, foghorn-like sounds. Although other fingerings are possible, those given here were selected to obtain the highest potential consistency of timbre and intonation. Strictly speaking, these pitches are not harmonics; they are, rather, unfocused and spread tones resulting from the closing of holes below the one open hole which produces a given pitch.

In my notations, (tr) indicates a trill, Th, 2, 3, 4 and 5 refer to the fingers. Letters in parentheses indicate keys to be depressed, and (½) signifies that the key is to be closed but the hole left open. The third of my *Movements for Three Flutes* develops these sonorities as the basic sound-material with, I feel, electrifying effect. This movement concludes, incidentally, with a sustained low B♭—a scordature pitch obtained by pulling the headjoint out about one inch and playing low B. (The player needs about four seconds in which to do this safely.) The tone is soft, round and, if played non vibrato, quite beautiful.

Finally, and for lack of a better place in which to mention it, there are many flutists who have excellent control of "whistle tones"—the·very soft, high, and extraordinarily clear pitches obtained by extremely gentle blowing across the blowhole.[6] The pitches are overtones of a fundamental (generally low B, C, or C♯) in the region of the fifth to tenth partials.

III. Noise Elements in the Tone

One of the earliest sounds in this now very broad category is the swoosh-like effect in the Villa-Lobos duo for flute and cello entitled *The Jet-Whistle*

[5] Bartolozzi's fingerings go down only to G♯.
[6] According to Harvey Sollberger, the flutist Robert Cantrick is expert at this.

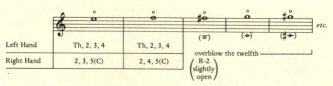

Left Hand	Th, 2, 3, 4	Th, 2, 3, 4	Th, 2, 3, 4	Th, 2, 3, 4	Th, 2, 3, 4(½)	Th, 2, 3, 4, 5
Right Hand	2, 3, 4(½), 5(C♯)	2, 3, 5(C & B)	2(½), 3, 4	3, 4, 5(C)	2, 3, 4, 5(C♯)	2, 3

Left Hand	Th, 2, 3(½), 4	Th, 2, 4	overblow the octave —————————————
Right Hand		2, 3	

Left Hand	Th, 2, 3, 4	Th, 2, 3, 4	overblow the twelfth ———————
Right Hand	2, 3, 5(C)	2, 4, 5(C)	(R-2 slightly open)

Ex. 2. For the flute: fingering for low-register harmonics

(1953). The flutist closes his entire mouth over the blowhole, fingers low B, and blows a sudden burst of air. One can discern the overtones of this B descending rapidly from about the eighth partial, but the strongest impression after the attack is that of air—a quick, white-noise-like, downward glissando resulting from the performer's rapid exhalation. A number of related sounds are obtainable through similar procedures. A master of these techniques is David Gilbert, whose astonishing *Poem VI* (1966) for alto flute sounds like an electronic piece and must be seen performed to be believed.

Joyce Mekeel, a composer and teaching colleague of mine in Boston, has a solo flute piece entitled *The Shape of Silence* (1969) in which spoken words, sharply enunciated, are used both to articulate and to sustain low-register tones (see Ex. 3). This work calls also for sotto voce tones of barely audible pitch with a predominantly wind-like sound, which are obtained by blowing rapidly *across* rather than into the blowhole. The composer neatly elides a sung tone with a played one in the passage quoted in Ex. 4. Readers are advised that for simultaneous production of sung and played tones, the flute's pitches are best placed in the low register.[7]

---

[7] The earliest example known to me of simultaneous playing and singing on the flute is by Sam Most on a jazz LP from the 1950's entitled *The Herbie Mann-Sam Most Quintet* (Bethlehem, No. BCP-40).

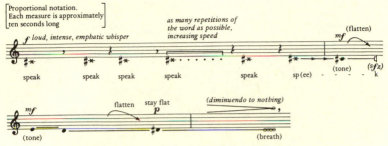

Ex. 3. From Mekeel, *The Shape of Silence*

Ex. 4. From Mekeel, *The Shape of Silence*

IV. New Multiple-Sonorities

The multiple-sonorities given in Ex. 5 are offered as additions to those listed in the two articles mentioned on page 207. The total content of these three lists for flute constitutes the current extent of my solid information in this area. Many additional sounds are no doubt possible; however, I have submitted only those which I feel are relatively secure as to intonation and ease of production.

As a final note, I hardly need emphasize the viability of the foregoing techniques for new music. Receptive performers consistently prove that the new techniques are easily learned and assimilated, and the effective integration of such techniques into works by composers as diverse as Martino, Johnston, Perle, Schuller, W. O. Smith, Paul Zonn, and those mentioned herein is testimony to their proliferation and vitality.

JOHN C. HEISS

○ = long or short duration

● = short duration only

↟ = trill the indicated finger(s)

21 / 22 / 23 / 24 / 25 / 26 26a

	21	22	23	24	25	26, 26a
Left Hand	Th, 2, 4	Th, 2, 3, 4	Th, 2, 3, 4	Th, 2, 3, 4(½)	Th, 2, 3(½), 4	2, 3, 4
Right Hand	2, 3, 4, 5(B)	2, 3(½), 4, 5(C)	2(½), 3, 4, 5(C♯)	2, 3, 4, 5(C)	2, 3, 4	4(½)

27 27a 28 29 (automatic flutter) 30 31 32 33 33a

	27, 27a	28	29	30	31	32	33, 33a
Left Hand	Th, 3	Th(B♭), 2, 4	Th, 3, 4, 5	Th, 3	Th, 2, 4	Th, 2	Th, 2, 4
Right Hand	2, 5(E♭)	2(tr), 3, 4	2, 3(tr)	4(tr)	2, 4(tr)	2(E), 3(tr), 4	4(tr), 5(E♭)

34 34a 34b 35 35a 35b 36 36a 36b

	34, 34a, 34b	35, 35a, 35b	36, 36a, 36b
Left Hand	Th, 3	Th, 2	Th, 2, 3, 4
Right Hand	2(tr)	4(tr)	2, 3, 5(C♯)

37 38 39 40 41

	37	38	39	40	41
Left Hand	Th, 2 ←	Th, 2, 3, 4, 5	Th, 2, 3	Th, 3, 4, 5	Th, 3, 4
Right Hand	2(tr), 3	2, 3, 4, 5(E♭)	2(tr), 3(tr),		2

separate and random trill-action   (joint trill-action)

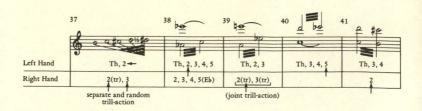

Ex. 5. Multiple-sonorities for flute (to be added to those listed on pp. 115–16 and 183)